I Prayed and Everything

Estrell Young III

(handwritten: midst of the vast darkness. Thank you for everything!)

I PRAYED AND EVERYTHING PUBLISHING

DECATUR, GA

Manufactured in the United States of America

Estrell Young III/I Prayed and Everything Publishing
Lithonia, GA 30058
www.estrellyoungIII.com

Publisher's Note: This is a work of autobiographical nonfiction. Names, characters, places, and incidents are not a product of the author's imagination but somethings have been changed for the purposes of this book. Locales and/or public names used are just for atmospheric purposes.

Library of Congress Cataloging-in-Publication Data is available.

I Prayed and Everything/ Estrell Young III -- 1st ed.
ISBN 978-0-1976100840

10 9 8 7 6 5 4 3 2 1

From: _____

To: _____

For Ivor Brooks
I love you, Chief

I Prayed and Everything

But my life is worth nothing to me unless I use it for finishing the work assigned me by the Lord Jesus—the work of telling others the Good News about the wonderful grace of God.

—Acts 20:24

3 Commit to the Lord whatever you do, and HE will establish your plans. **—Proverbs 16:3 (NIV)**

Table of Contents

It Won't Be There

Chapter One
Car Trouble

Stupid is as stupid does. This, a famous quote from the movie Forrest Gump, in part, describes my childhood because I did some incredibly stupid things.

"Boy, go back and close that door!"

The screen slammed loudly behind me but I ignored it. More scared than hurt, my body pulsed from the chemicals my emotions caused to course through my veins. Terrified, I didn't have time to mind small, common courtesy's like not interrupting people while they were talking and closing doors to ensure I was not air conditioning the "entire neighborhood" like my mom suggested I had been known to do. A car ran over me. Nothing else mattered.

"You know you wrong, right?" grandpa said, sitting on the couch shifting his attention back and forth between his new Nixon F-601 and the manual.

"Whatever," aunt T snapped back as if she had lost her cotton-pick'n mind.

As I walked down the hallway, snail-like toward the living room, I knew something was wrong. My grandma normally peered down the hall to make sure we took off our shoes. She would say, "This carpet cost'd us a fortune." But not this time. Nothing. She didn't look for me. I was lucky to be alive and no one had a clue.

"Whatever, huh? Who do you think you're talking to?" grandpa tested, moving to the edge of the chair and shooting a glance toward the kitchen.

"I bought it because I can afford it now. You should be happy. Now you won't have to worry about me bothering you to work on it every three months."

"That's not what I'm talking about and you know it."

I inched into the room, waiting to make my presence known but frightened at the same time.

"I have no problem with your getting a new car. It's the way you went about it that I don't agree with."

Ahhhhhh they're arguing about aunt T's new car. Another injection of fear took hold and I began to panic all over again.

"I said go back and close that door, boy. You're not paying any bills round here," my mom shouted snapping me back to reality. Again, not even one look in my direction.

I was not seriously injured but I couldn't seem to catch my breath. I was bloody and covered in oil. Scraped and scratched up. I was glad too because I thought my family would feel sorry for me and, maybe, not care so much about the car.

"Tell me. What did I do that was so bad, Dad?" She shifted in her chair, seeming like she'd grown impatient with the conversation.

Even though I was a child, I could feel the tension in the room and I could tell my aunt knew exactly what my grandpa was talking about. *You only get frustrated when you're caught.* My mom taught me that. We all knew what she did. Grandpa had been fussing all morning about how he was going to give Auntie a 'piece of his mind' when she got back from the dealership.

This was my moment. I stepped forward and tears began to flow more abundantly. As I stood in the doorway crying, no one noticed. I was crying so hard that the only sound I made was short, quick, gasps for air. Tears streamed down my face so freely, I could swear a small puddle formed beneath my feet. I was putting on a show. When my grandma saw me, and my mother came running that's when I shifted into high gear. I wailed loudly.

"Estrell! Baby, what happen to you? Oh, my God!"

"I...I...I..." I couldn't form a sentence.

"Are you okay?" Grandma asked as she rushed over, reaching through my mother's arms to console me.

"Baby, tell me what happen! Where were you playing? Take me to where you got hurt," she pleaded while looking me over.

"But it won't be there."

"What won't be there, Estrell? Take me to where you got hurt!"

"The car."

In unison, my mother, aunt, and grandmother, who had all been sitting at the kitchen table sipping coffee said, "What car?"

"The car," I said again, wiping my eye and looking up from the floor.

"Whose car? Estrell, were you hit by a car!?"

With all eyes on me, I pointed at aunt T. A collection gasp silenced the room then all the adults took off out the door. I followed behind slowly. There was no need for me to run. I already knew what the scene looked like.

"Oh, no!" aunt T cried, as she disappeared outside.

Chapter Two
Shaken

Aunt T, which was short for Tabitha, was a devout Christian. She introduced my sister and me to God by dragging us to church whenever it was open—bible study, revival, Sunday school, prayer meetings, you name it—if the door was open, we were in the building. And she could scream and shout, praise and worship with the best of them. There wasn't a service where she didn't cry. Afterwards, she would take us to Dairy Queen and buy us treats.

I love Aunt T. I love her more than a dipped cone with extra sprinkles. I love her so much that when I exited the house, I stood off to the side while everyone else huddled at the top of the driveway, mouths gaping, looking confused. Their sheer disbelief caused shame to set in.

"Sweet baby Jesus," my mother muttered, covering her mouth.

There it was, my auntie's, fresh off the lot, '91 sapphire blue Toyota Camry ruined. The brand-new smell inside. The sticker still taped to the window mocking her. Her pride and joy sitting smashed and pinned to a tree across the street. She hadn't even made the first payment.

My aunt stepped towards the wreckage. "But that's my car!"

"What in the world happen to it?" Grandma could be a little slow at times.

"That's what you get for being greedy," Grand-pa added. He had given my aunt a car that she drove into the ground before buying this new one.

"What?" Aunt T spun around in disbelief.

"This is karma. I told you. You had no business trying to sell your cousins a car that wasn't yours to sell. And you're supposed to be God-fearing. What kind of child of God does something like that, huh? I'd say he's trying to teach you a lesson."

"I told them I'd give them the freaking car! What else do you want me to do?"

"Then why do you still have it, Tab?"

"I just put a full tank of gas in there!"

"Exactly. You're going to give them that car on E. We raised you better than that."

I prayed silently. God, how do I tell them? How do I tell them that I accidently knocked the car out of gear while I was playing racecar driver on grandpa's motor speedway? God, how do I—

"Are y'all going to stand there all day or is someone going to get that car out of the neighbor's yard?"

My grandpa was a straight shooter. And he had a point. Someone needed to make a move.

"But how? It's all smashed up."

This was my second, and possibly worst, mistake of the day. I was too smart for my own britches. They had all but forgotten about me and I had to open my big mouth.

Aunt T spun around then closed the gap between us with two steps.

"What did you do?" Her body eclipsed the Sun and casted a shadow around me in all directions. She panted. She fumed with rage. Smoke billowed from her ears. Her eyes fixed on mine like a heat-seeking missile. She was shaking. "What did you do?"

"I, uh…"

"I'm going to kill you." Aunt T snatched me up like a ragdoll and rung me so hard I felt my brain slosh around in my skull.

This was the Tabitha I had come to know. Not the church-going Christian, but the quick-tempered, easily angered, and, more often than not, unreasonable Auntie T. She could be mean.

I had developed a love/hate relationship with her because she would pinch me for sleeping in church. I hated being pinched. My inability to sit still, be quiet, and conform to her expectations made things worse. She would either thump my ear for the slightest misstep. She often told me there was a special place in Hell for little boys like me.

My grandfather shouted, "Put that boy down. This ain't his fault. Who left the car unlocked? The car wouldn't have been in the driveway if you hadn't been so greedy."

She put me down with such force my knees buckled and I fell forward on the pavement.

"But, Daddy ..."

This moment in time symbolizes one of my earliest memories of church and religion. Ironically, it had nothing to do with either. It had everything to do with the person who introduced me to them.

Looking back, I have always believed God is real. I don't know why but I did. Even so, I stopped going to church when my family stopped forcing me to. I had a tough time separating the behavior of one Christian from the institution. Maybe I was too young to know I was supposed to.

Marbut Elementary

Chapter Three
Change sucks

"Estrell, I know you're awake. Shake a leg!" Mom shouted as she tossed a washcloth and towel both of which land squarely upon my head.

"Mom, how do you know I be up?"

"When the snoring stops, baby," she chuckled. A smile overtook her face. She didn't smile much, so when it happened you noticed.

My mom was a hard-working woman. She began this morning, same as every other morning, on her knees in the living room, towering over the mini ironing board, preparing my clothes for the day. Everything she would do looked effortless and easy. She took pride in my sister and me. This was clear in the way she carefully ran the iron along the length of my trousers, perfect from crease to cuff, and the way she would spend hours in the bathroom battling my sister's kinky hair.

"No child of mine is walking out of the house looking like a ragamuffin," she would say.

Our one-bedroom efficiency was cozy, but there wasn't much privacy. Painted the color of creamed corn, it was situated right next to the elevator. It was noisy, but we had grown used to the creak of the doors and whine of the cables. These arrangements were only temporary though. Last week, Mom closed on a house near my new school. We'll be moving soon.

I watched her through the mirror. The occasional sip of coffee from her favorite mug and a loving gaze shot my way as I washed my face, served as a break from her labor.

"Now, listen. It took a lot of money, time, and a miracle from God to get you in-

to this school. Don't you go up in there act-
ing no damn fool, you hear me?"

"Yes, ma'am," I replied, scrubbing away
at my cheeks.

"I'm not playing with you, boy."

"I hear you, jeez."

"And you better not mess up your new
clothes. Your grandfather and I had to hus-
tle two Vietnamese seamstresses for those."

My new uniform: two embroidered po-
los—navy and white—with my new school
logo; two pairs of khakis—tan and navy—
and a pair of all-black non-designer shoes,
all of which was a topic of great contention
with Mom. Clearly, it stressed her out. She
wouldn't stop talking about how the clothes
had to be ordered and specially made. Apparently, just finding a company that could
make what I needed was a nightmare. And
to make matters worse, the clothes were ex-
pensive. Hear her tell it, my uniform cost 'an
arm and a leg,' though, I'm still curious as to
where she acquired the limbs to this day. I
had no sympathy for her, though. All of this
was her fault.

"Are you excited?"

"I guess."

"You guess!? You're going to be in the first graduating class from this school, Estrell. They'll probably have your picture on the wall and everything!"

"None of my friends are going to be there. Tee, Skip, Dre, and Ced are all staying at Pine Lake," I counted in dismay, as if holding up the four fingers were the icing on this colossal cake of apprehension.

"You'll make new friends, honey."

"I don't want new friends," I mumbled. *She can't be serious? New friends?* "I mean its fourth grade for heaven's sake. These next two years are supposed to be an important time for us because we'll be upperclassmen, you know? I mean, I'm not sure if there is such a thing for elementary school but…"

I walked over to the couch, which also served as my bed, tossed the wool brownie-colored cushions to the floor in disgust and withdrew a photograph. My class picture from third grade. I'd had each of my friends sign it, and we swore we would be best friends forever. I began to sob.

My mom sat back on her feet. "Hey, come here." She placed her willowy arms around me and said, "I'm sorry you won't get to go to school with your friends, baby. But it's not like we're moving out of town. You'll be able to see them on the weekends and holidays. You may not understand it now, but this change is going to open a lot of doors for you; you just wait and see."

"This sucks."

∗ ∗ ∗

Two months into the school year and things weren't going so well...I'd been suspended twice, had a bout with lice, and I've spent so much time with the ISS teacher she knows me personally. How awesome is that? She could pronounce my name correctly and everything. My mother, however, wasn't impressed by my behavior. She cornered me in front of the bathing area.

"Estrell, today is your first day back in a regular class setting. You can't get in any more trouble, okay? You don't want those people labeling you as something you're not. Now go get your book bag. You're going to be late."

"Okay, Mom," I offered, violently rubbing my eye.

"And have you seen the box of matches I had on top of the television?"

"No, I haven't seen them," I answered, placing my book bag on the kitchen table.

"Are you sure? I remember seeing them up there before I went to bed."

I knew she was mistaken, though. *I had snatched those matches on Friday before I left, so there's no way she saw them on the TV last night.*

"Yep," I insisted, glancing into my backpack to ensure they were still just where I had stashed them. "Hey, do I have to go to school today? I'm really tired, and my eye itches."

It was a cold October morning. Mondays were the worst. The weekend had flown by much faster than usual, and I was nowhere near excited about having to go back to school so quickly.

"You're going to school."

"But Mom," I whined.

"This isn't a negotiation. And you can pout all you want, but you've already missed more days of regular class sessions than most kids miss in a year. Now go get your book bag and head out."

I grabbed my coat from the rack, opened the front door, and tried a very somber exit before I was halted.

"What? You're too mad to give your mom a kiss goodbye?"

Leaving the door cracked, I turned and walked over to her, rubbing my right eye vigorously.

"Stop that! I know what you're trying to do, and giving yourself a red eye isn't going to keep you from going to school." She hugged my pudgy body and sent me on my way.

Chapter Four
What are those?

Now let's back up for a minute. There are some things you should probably know about me before we get to the action. First, I was considered a bad kid. I don't think I leveled up to Dennis the Menace but, I was on the same scale. In kindergarten, I was sent home so much I had to repeat the grade. Who knew that could even happen? My mom recently informed me that, of the mountain of things I did to get kicked out, recoloring the multicolored alphabet carpet with blue paint was the straw that broke the camel's back. She went on to say that she had warned the administration after my fourth suspension that, upon my return, I'd either be reformed or even more supernaturally deviant. I chose the latter, and soon after, I was diagnosed with ADD and placed on a medication called Ritalin. It was not the best of times. The meds turned me into a zombie, and I remember being sad often.

Second, I was overweight. And not the "a smidge past chubby" type of fat either; I was wrapped in a layer of pudge too thick to belong to a baby. To make matters worse, my mother had no sense of style. With her, nothing was off the table. Seriously, Bill Cosby-style sweaters, corduroy pants, overalls, denim pant suits, and to top it off, my shoe game was atrocious. There is nothing more horrifying than finding out your J's are fake in the middle of a school day. Especially when you thought you were clean! Picture this. I was sitting in the bleachers, minding my own business, when a group of boys approached me.

"Yo, Estrell. Can we ask you a question?"

"That is a question," I quipped. I had seen this scene many times before. These guys would stroll up on unsuspecting victims and roast the life from them. No one was safe.

"Haha. Seriously."

"I'm listening," I replied.

"Well, we were all wondering..." The boy paused, and I could feel the gym grow quiet. What happened next can only be described as slow-motion cinematography. With an expressionless face, his gaze shifted downward toward my shoes, and he pointed. He then posed a question that was both equally dramatic and vicious.

"What are those?!"

The gym erupted into laughter in all directions. My peers went nuts; some collapsed to the floor and rolled around from the hysteria; others held their bellies, and a few wiped tears from their eyes because the chuckle was so great. Kids can be so cruel. I had never been so embarrassed, and I took it hard. My imitation J's had a basketball where the Jumpman should've been. So, when I got home, I tied the laces together and tossed them up on the power lines in front of my house. I vowed from that day forward I would never be victimized by guys like them again. I made it my mission to sharpen my ability to notice shortcomings and to talk crap. I became good too. Whenever and wherever I saw them, I was supremely disrespectful on sight, and no one was safe. This bit of information will be important later in the story, so remember it; moving on.

Third, I was brilliant. I read on an eighth-grade level. I could solve a Rubrik's cube in less than ten seconds and I taught myself how to ride a bike when I was five-years-old, just minutes of receiving my first one for Christmas. My mother recalls that I told my grandfather to "take that crap off" when he rolled it into the garage with training wheels affixed to the back. I guess I was a bit snappy too. My brilliance didn't stop there, though. I was also inclined creatively. I loved to write stories and draw. Oh, how I could draw! I convinced my entire family that I was this child prodigy with a pencil and a sketch pad, when I was really just tracing my butt off. I had it down to a science. It all came down to the transparency of the paper. One day, they asked me to draw in front of them while they watched, and the jig was up. Looking back now, I see that I had ignored my true talent, writing.

Fourth, and finally, I loved to learn. I was a sponge. I soaked up everything from National Geographic to this magazine I would regularly steal from the grocery store called Guns and Ammo. I am not proud of it, but I would stuff the newest issue in my waistline, underneath my shirt, and walk right out of the store. There is a lot of irony here. Career wise, I only wanted to be one of two things as a child—either a pilot or a policeman. Unfortunately, my dreams of soaring across the big blue sky were dashed when some seriously unimportant and negative person informed me that I had to have 20/20 vision to pilot. So, in my mind, it was settled—I'd be a police officer, one who stole. I am not sure where the call to serve came from, but it has been, along with varying degrees of law breaking, with me since an early age.

Chapter Five
Lies have legs

Fast-forward to the day everything changed. A typical Monday, other than a few skirmishes and a couple of failed attempts at thumb wrestling, the morning was uneventful. I was one of the first kids to finish the daily word search, so I sat at my desk quietly and folded hornets. Hornets are paper bullets you can shoot using a rubber band. I was stocking up on them because someone was going to be assassinated at lunch. My eye was itching nonstop. It was really beginning to bother me, and the vigorousness of my rubbing didn't help. I was about to raise my hand and inquire about some eyedrops when Ms. Linangrass summoned me.

"Estrell! Front and center, now."

"Huh?" I spun around. *What did I do? She must've seen the hornets.* I stuffed the twice-folded pieces of paper into my book bag and placed it under my seat. "Yes, ma'am?"

"Get up here."

"Coming," I said sheepishly. When Ms. Linangrass took a pointed tone with you, it was never good.

"Bring your book bag, too."

She was a stern but fair woman, short, and spry for her age. She had a kind face that matched her pearl necklace and long skirt. She almost dressed like a nun.

I walked toward her desk warily, passing by Tonya Spellman, who, unknown to me, had spoken with Ms. Linangrass just prior to my summoning. The class murmured and speculated about my offense and began to place bets on my fate. Anxiety crept up my body from my shoes. I rubbed my hand on the leg of my pants to wick away the sweat.

Ms. Linangrass handed me a pink slip which I reluctantly grabbed.

"What's this for?"

"I am sending you to the principal's office for bringing a weapon to school."

I shot a piercing look at Tonya, who was at her desk, the biggest grin on her face. I was at once outraged and bewildered. I was just minding my own business. "What do you mean? I don't know what you're talking about," I shouted angrily. I was puzzled. It was one thing to be punished for something I did, but I wasn't about to let her punish me for something I'm not sure she had any knowledge of. "Ms. Linangrass, those are just paper footballs. They travel farther when you fold them like that," I explained, showing her my book bag. She was unmoved, and for good reason.

Without hesitation, Tonya Spellman, my arch nemesis, stood up and yelled what, to me, sounded like a clear and definite checkmate, "And he threatened to kill me, too." She was beaming ear-to-ear, and I truly did want to kill her right then. As much as I hated to admit it, part of her statement was true, but the other part was a bold-faced lie, so I did what any self-respecting eight-year-old would do—denied harder.

26

"You're a liar!" I shouted back furiously, even though name-calling could potentially get you a few days of detention. And Tonya stuck her tongue out.

"That's it." Ms. Linangrass seized my ear, and practically dragged my plump behind out of class. "Tell it to the principal." She pushed me far enough into the hall so she could shut the door in my face. Inside the room, I could hear the taunts and catcalls of my so-called friends. They were chanting "Estrell's going to get it" over and over as I trudged down the hall. I was in shock, but I couldn't wallow in it because I had to get my story straight for the principal. I walked very slowly.

The front wall of the front office was made up of a series of window panes, and then the door. The admin staff could see you coming from down the hall if they were paying attention. When I reached the middle, I pressed my face against the glass like how inmates do when peering out of their cells. The secretary gestured for me to come in. The door to Mrs. Richards's office was open, and she was standing in the doorway glaring at me. It was obvious that Ms.

Linangrass had phoned ahead and told her of my imminent arrival.

"Hand me your book bag."

I didn't have a choice but to hand her my bag, but I made no effort to do it quickly. I wasn't worried because I didn't have a weapon. The most she would find would be the "paper footballs" and some matches I lifted from my mom the week prior.

"Mrs. Richards, I didn't threaten Tonya; she's just mad because I said she had some saggy titties, and maybe I joked a little too much about her looking like curious George. But I didn't say nothing about hurting her. She's a bully. She terrorizes the other kids because she likes to see them cry."

"Put the bag on the desk and open it up."

I continued, "And that bothered me. Every time I would see her I'd say, "Why, good morning, George! Or Tonya! What mighty long gorilla arms you have! But I never said I'd kill her. That's not true, Mrs. Richards." I was babbling, and I knew it, but I couldn't help it.

Mrs. Richards wasn't paying me any attention. Her focus was on my book bag. She scoured the contents of my bag, combing through hornets, other random sheets of loose-leaf paper, and books. As my eyes followed hers, my heart sank in my chest. *Dang it, the knife!* My eye began to itch again, and I could feel panic begin to set in. I had forgotten all about the orange retractable box cutter. That, along with the matches and the small Nerf gun I had thrown in my book bag that past weekend could spell disaster. I figured I should head her off at the pass.

"Mrs. Richards, wait. There's a box cutter in there. We had our annual church camping trip in the North Georgia Mountains over the weekend, and I just threw some stuff in there trying to look cool. It was a horrible experience. First, I left my sleeping bag at home in the middle of the living room floor, so I had to sleep on the ground inside the tent. Second, apart from the insect bites, it was freezing! Do you know how cold it gets at night in the mountains? Two of my toes were still thawing as of this morning. Third, as you might've guessed, I didn't get any sleep. So, you can see how the knife being in my book bag could be an honest mistake, right?"

Mrs. Richards paused; this was very dramatic on her part. She slowly began to withdraw her hand from the innards of my bag, and I held my breath.

"This knife?"

"Yup. That's it."

"I'll be keeping this," she bragged.

"You're confiscating it?"

"Yes. Do you know what that means?"

"Yeah, you're taking it."

"Correct," she sighed. "Go wait in my office."

Mrs. Richards was old-school. She reminded me of Joe Clark, played by Morgan Freeman in the movie *Lean on Me*. Recently divorced, she had made the success of Marbut her mission. She sat on the desk and pulled the phone close. Her face was one of disappointment, even though she never made mention of the toy gun or the matches. "Now I have to call your mother."

Well, that's not so bad. It wouldn't be the first time mom was called to come up to the school for something I had done. As long as they don't call grandpa, I'm good. I grabbed my book bag off the desk and slinked into her office. I climbed up on the leather couch by the window and, relieved, thought about the bullet I had just dodged. I could hear Mrs. Richards on the phone with my mother. For some reason, she talked to her while on speaker-phone.

"Good morning, Ms. Young. This is Mrs. Richards from Marbut Theme School."

"Good morning."

"We have Estrell here in the office with us. It seems he brought a box cutter to school with him this morning."

"Fudge."

"Excuse me?"

I could hear my mother's sigh. It was one of those sighs where you could tell things were beginning to be too much. "So, what happens now?"

"Well, he'll have to spend the rest of the day up here with us, and we will call you later this afternoon once we've come up with the best course of action, okay?"

"Okay."

"Do you want to speak to him?"

"No. He knows what's coming."

I sank down in the chair and continued where I had left off rubbing my eye. Mrs. Richards hung up the phone, walked back in, tossed the box cutter on her desk, and headed straight for me.

"What are we going to do with you, young man?"

"I don't know," I replied, raising my shirt to do the job my fingers couldn't.

"Stop that! Put your shirt down. Nobody wants to see all that."

"Sorry. My eye itches."

"Let me see." She reached out and grabbed my chin. Instinctively, I pulled back. "Hold still." Mrs. Richards turned my head to the right and then to the left before turning it back to the right again." Boy, how long has your eye been like this?"

"Like what?"

"Red!"

"It's red? I don't know, but it has been bothering me since last night."

"I think you might have pink eye. This changes everything. You might have to go home now. I need you to go to the nurse's office and keep your fingers out of your eyes."

"Can I go to the bathroom first?"

"Yes, but go and come right back. Pink eye is contagious. And wash your hands!"

"Okay."

I grabbed my book bag and jumped off the chair, excited for the opportunity to explore something new. I had never been inside the nurse's office. It was right across the hall from the principal's office, but it just didn't seem like the kind of place you would wander into, unless something was wrong, of course.

Chapter Six
Ashes Dance Too

When I got to the boys' bathroom, the door was locked. I pushed on it several times to make sure, and I guess the noise I was making could be heard down the hall. Coach Adams, our assistant principal, came out of his office to take a look.

"Estrell, what are you doing?"

Yes, he knew my name too. I was popular. What can I say?

"Mrs. Richards said I could use the bathroom."

"That one is locked. Come use mine."

I trotted down the hall to his office. I walked in, and he pointed toward the door to his personal bathroom. It was all clean and nice smelling on account of it being new and all. Just as I began to close the door, someone called for him over the walkie-talkie. *Coach Adams, we need you in the lunch room.* I turned and looked at him, and he looked at me.

"I have to run. Close the door when you're finished."

"Okay."

The assistant principal left me alone in the room, with no supervision. In essence, what happened next was all his fault. He knew I couldn't be trusted. I went into the bathroom, closed the door, and locked it.

After using it, which I really did have to do, I flushed and washed my hands. I played with the bubbles in the sink for a few minutes before emptying most of Coach Adams's Wild-Berry Deep-Cleansing Hand Soap into the trash, and then, I remembered the matches. I went to the door, peeked out to make sure the coast was clear, and retrieved the matches from my bag. At first, I was content with burning holes in the toilet paper. I didn't mean to start a fire, okay? I just liked the smell of freshly-lit matches, and the way stuff shriveled up when you set a match to it.

The jumbo rolls of *Novex* commercial toilet paper Marbut Theme School stockpiled in closets next to the bathrooms sucked. They were super-thin and rough, probably single ply as sometimes your fingers poked through as you wiped, but Coach Adams had the good stuff. It had to be Charmin. The first couple of sheets went up nicely; their ashes floating like snowflakes dancing on a breeze. As you can see, I meant to burn the tissue. I had a whole box of matches to play with, and it offered a small rush of adrenaline. The small holes weren't going to hurt nobody. But, I didn't mean to set anything on fire, if that makes sense.

The toilet paper was okay. It did its job. But the party started when I moved to paper towels. Paper towels took things to a whole other level. In my genius mind, I figured this could easily get out of hand, so I had the bright idea to pile them in the sink so I could manage the situation if this became one. I snatched fistfuls from the dispenser and stacked them just below the lip of the sink. Without so much as a blink, I struck the first match and went to drop it on top of the paper, but the flame went out. I think that was God telling me to stop with the foolishness. I ignored him. I lit another. The towels went up quicker than I expected, almost as if they were flammable. Heaps of brown smoke filled the bathroom, and it freaked me out. I turned on the faucet, put out the flames, and began throwing the leftover paper in the trash. I turned on the fan to try and get rid of the smoke. I'd had enough excitement for one day. I finished cleaning the sink, and started back to my original destination, the nurse's office. The bathroom was still smoky when I opened the door. Did I mention this was a brand-new school, and that the bathroom was inside the assistant principal's office, right down the hall from the front office? Well, it was, and some smoke had made it into the hallway. I didn't know this at the time, but the principal assumed the smoke was electrical in nature, and called the fire department before pulling the alarm. I was hiding in the nurse's office when the siren sounded. The school was evacuated and we were all ushered, herd-like, into the parking lot. All my friends, even that baboon Tonya, were out there, and it was like having recess but without the snack. I was so excited, I forgot about my part in all of this.

It wasn't until I saw the fire marshal, Coach Adams, and the principal together talking that I realized my little butt would soon be the focus of their investigation. I tossed the matches under a car and circled around to the other side of the parking lot. I reentered the school with the rest of the student body and parked myself in the nurse's office. It wasn't long before Mrs. Richards was in the doorway; the disappointed look on her face had given way to anger.

"Come."

I grabbed my book bag and followed behind quietly. Firefighters found the burnt paper towels in the bathroom trash can, and since I was the last person in Coach Adams's bathroom, I was the prime suspect. We walked into the front office, and everyone stared. No one said or asked me anything. Coach A just pointed to a chair.

* * *

When the principal called my mother this time, it wasn't as social. Instead of suggesting, she insisted my mom come get me at once. In fact, I had to wait outside for her. Needless to say, I got suspended for the rest of the year pending a review by the Board of Education. Oddly enough, they still allowed me to complete my assignments. My mother would pick up and drop off my schoolwork every Friday, and even though I had no teacher to teach me, I was able to keep a three-point-something GPA and move on to the next grade. That was good news.

The school board meeting was on the last official day of the school year, and it didn't go so well. The witness list was lengthy. It was like they flew people in to testify about how deviant I was. Even Tonya joined the circus. She came and testified, and made the lie stronger that started this roller coaster and was, certainly, the final knife in my coffin. My mom cried the whole time. I was furious. The board wouldn't give us their decision that day, but I assumed the worst.

It would be three weeks before we heard anything.

A month or so passed since the school board meeting, and my mom had been giving me the silent treatment. I could tell she was disappointed, but there was nothing I could do about it, except pray. As much as I hated Tonya, I wanted to be able to go back to school. I couldn't take another week with my grandparents. They didn't let me watch television or nothing. It was hell. I was sitting in my room when I heard the front door slam in our otherwise quiet house. Intrigued, I opened my door. My mom was just staring at the floor. A white envelope dangled from her fingers.

"What's wrong?"

Her face was a mixture of emotions. Fear, anger, and maybe a little resolve.

"It's official. They don't want you back."

"Who?" I had no idea what she was talking about.

"Don't play dumb, Estrell. Marbut is not having you back. In fact, you've been kicked out of the district and have to go to alternative school. You have to go to Hamilton."

My chest became heavy. My breathing labored, the sensation of drowning overtook my body. I frantically looked around for a life vest and shot off a thousand questions.

"Stop playing. What do you mean? Are they serious? They don't want me back because of a little smoke? How do you know? Did they call? We just went to court like yesterday? Where is Hamilton?"

"They sent a letter in the mail, genius."

"How could it get here that fast?"

"What difference does it make? Obviously, they had their minds made up before we even left court. This letter is dated the day before your hearing."

"But I can't go to Hamilton. Don't you know they kill people in there?"

"You should have thought about that before you got expelled. It's out of my hands now."

I felt like I was living a bad dream, and all I wanted to do was wake up. I had never really given much thought to going to alternative school because I never fathomed this situation being that serious. "Can I see the letter?" My mom was good at tricking me, and I was praying this was just a terrible prank.

She walked up to me and pushed the letter into my chest. This was when I realized how serious this situation was. Without even reading the letter, I cried.

"Mom, I swear I'm innocent."

"For what it's worth, I believe you had no intention of hurting anyone, and this is a big misunderstanding. However, perception is everything. That's why I told you not to give those people any reason to judge you."

"I'm sorry."

"My worst nightmare for you is coming true. Despite everything I've done, you are going to have to lie in the bed you made. Heaven help you." Mom turned, walked down the hall to her bedroom, and closed the door. I could hear her sobbing, and for a moment, I wanted to comfort her. I tried her door, but it was locked. Sliding down the length of the door, we cried together.

Chapter Seven
Out of place

When I got off the bus, there was a line at the door. My book bag was heavy, my palms soaking the polyester straps and dampening my clothes; I was scared. Hamilton was not a normal school by any stretch of the imagination. It looked like a scene from *Dangerous Minds*. There were metal detectors just inside the entrance; droves of small adults inching their way forward to be searched. Kids standing off to the side jostling, with hand-to-hand exchanges to evade arrest for contraband; girls distracting the guards for their boyfriends with their short skirts and accidental wardrobe malfunctions. *Toto, I have a feeling we're not in Kansas anymore.* This is going to be interesting.

"Hey babe, how was your first day?"

"Eventful."

"What's that supposed to mean?"

"I don't belong there, mom."

"What happened?"

"Well, when I got off the bus, which was an experience because all the kids who ride that particular bus are special needs, except me, we had to pass through metal detectors and be searched by guards because that teacher got murdered by a student last year. Then, the whole school meets in the cafeteria for breakfast before homeroom."

"How was that?"

"Ummmm...it was crowded."

"I bet."

"There weren't a lot of chairs or space, so I stood. I watched this one kid who was lucky enough to find a seat. He placed his stuff down and positioned his chair to show that it was his, and then he got in line for food. While he was in line, another guy who had gotten his food came and moved the first boy's stuff and took his chair."

"That's not cool."

"I know, right? The boy wasn't too happy about it when he came back and discovered his stuff had been moved and his seat had been taken."

"So, what did he do?"

"Calm down, Mom. I'm going to tell you."

"Sorry."

"He tapped the boy on the shoulder and pointed out to him that his stuff was there; he had just jumped in line to get breakfast, and that he had sat in his seat. The other boy told him he didn't see his name on it, so he wasn't going to get up."

"Wow. Then what happened?"

"The first boy put his tray down and then pulled the chair out from under the other boy, who fell to the ground."

"You're kidding!"

"Nope."

"But it's just the first day of school..."

"I was thinking the same thing."

"Did they fight?"

"Yeah, Mom. It turned into a brawl. People were throwing food and chairs; standing up on tables and pushing people down. It was a mess."

"What did you do?"

"The only thing I could do. I threw food too!"

"Estrell!"

After a year, I returned to regular school, just not Marbut Elementary. I learned a lot in my time away; picture inmates communing with likeminded individuals in cellblocks across this great country. I got my taste of underworld and I didn't like it. But probably not for the reasons you may thinking. Alternative school was an unbelievably humbling experience because the underlying theme of all our stories were the same; we were all lost, struggling to cope with the cards dealt to us and society had excommunicated us. We were unwanted and that feeling, along with the thoughts that came with it, stuck with me moving forward.

Terrible Choices

Chapter Eight
Would you like some water?

Sitting in the foyer of the Campus Center of my alma mater, I can't believe someone actually convinced me to come back here. After I graduated, I swore to myself I would never set foot in Carrollton again for as long as I lived. But now that I'm here...there's a wide range of emotions coming back all at once. *This place wasn't that bad.*

Outside of this building, major renovations have changed the landscape, but the facelift didn't rebuild the bones. We all know there's still a one-hundred-year-old woman behind the plaster and caulk. A young girl, maybe twenty, methodically climbs the monstrous indoor rock wall. Her patience is as impressive as this wall, which wasn't here ten years ago. A murmur fills the air, and it smells like endless possibilities. Students and faculty coming and going in all directions. When I was here, we thought we had nothing but time. Realizing that you don't is a bitter pill to swallow. I remember the hardest question ever posed to me was: 'What are you going to be when you grow up?' *I hope no one recognizes me.*

"Mr. Young, Mr. Daniels will be right with you. Would you like some water while you wait?"

"No. I'm fine. Thank you."

Next to me was a portly fellow, mid-thirties, wearing light green pajama bottoms and a gray *ThunderCats* T-shirt. He was reading *Crime and Punishment* by Dostoevsky.

"She didn't offer me any water," he grumbled, never looking up from his book.

"Are you waiting for Mr. Daniels too?"

"No, but I am thirsty."

I got up and walked over to the receptionist. She was cute, shoulder-length hair the color of autumn, sandy-brown eyes, and a drawl.

"Yes?"

"I'd actually like that water if the offer still stands."

She rolled her chair back from the desk and over to a mini-fridge next to the copier. She retrieved two bottles of *Deer Park* from it and slid back.

"I just wanted one."

"This one is for me," she responded, placing the one bottle on the desk and handing the other to me.

"Thanks."

I walked back to the salmon-colored divan and handed off the bottled water. The guy looked at me graciously, but I knew what it meant.

"You didn't have to do that."

"I know," I assured him as I sat back down.

In that moment, it was difficult to articulate the gravity of how I was feeling. I was being stretched—beads of sweat formed on my forehead; my palms were clammy, and my stomach somersaulted. *I don't know why I feel this way: nostalgic, nervous, and nauseous.* This institution, nestled here in the deep rural south, had cemented within me a couple of things. One, a narrative: one group of people is and always will be better than some others; that there is a ranking system, tiers if you will, which suggest one's place. In sociology, I learned of terms like agency and white spaces. Places, like this one, which make me uncomfortable because of Webster's definitions of 'black'— *opposite from white, and/or thoroughly sinister and evil.* Color is how 'they' see us. And I had bought in— hook, line, and sinker because it was Webster's dictionary! I never contemplated the motives of the author of a dictionary. I never even imagined authors, who told us the meanings of words, could be pawns in a system perpetuating such a coercive narrative. Dictionaries were sacrosanct to me.

Yesterday, I was sitting in court waiting for the judge to call a case I had worked on. A private attorney, defending a young man, stood in front arguing his position regarding the man's possible sentence. He argued that his client, who had merely made a poor choice, was still young—seventeen— salvageable, not too far gone, not a lost cause. And it broke my heart. *Salvageable? You mean, like a '63 Chevy?* I had committed the same crime in my youth. Yet, and still, here I am, sitting, waiting here, because of my love of words. I wanted desperately to tell that young man he was valuable.

"Are you interviewing for a job or something?" the man asked. He closed his book, sat it down beside him, and began to sip from the bottle. Obviously, he was ready for a chat.

"Nope. The school paper is doing an article one me. I used to go here, and they're curious about what I'm up to now."

"Nice. Did you graduate?"

"Yeah," I said as I glanced down at my watch to hide my dissatisfaction with his question.

"Nice. What year? If you don't mind me asking, and what did you get your degree in?"

"2009. I received my BS in Criminology."

"Nice. Do you work in the same field as your degree?"

"Yeah."

* * *

I looked at the door to Mr. Daniels's office and tried to use my mind to draw him out. It didn't work.

"What do you do?"

"I am a criminal defense investigator with the Dekalb County Public Defender's Office."

"Nice; sounds neat. You look important." He picked up the book and held it. "Dostoevsky once said, 'There are chance meetings with strangers that interest us from the first moment, before a word is spoken.' "

"Does my presence pique your interest, sir?"

The other narrative that had taken root within me, since I'm thinking about its stupidity, was: I am a problem, an issue to resolve, a demographic to be handled, a car to salvaged from some unthinkable fate—disposable. Apparently, I bought into this as well. I sold drugs during my time here. I got a DUI, too. Hell, the reason I even chose this school did more to convince me 'they' were right, than my intent to pursue higher education. *I think I am going to be sick.* Somehow, I had the audacity to believe, despite my past, because I graduated from college I was better than anyone who didn't. Because I was no longer considered poor and had obtained gainful employment, I wasn't the *black people* 'they' were referring to when conversing about folks across the railroad tracks. It is here, in this foyer, amidst my own self-inspection and reflection, I finally came to understand the heinous and incendiary effect racism has had on me. What great irony! I had subconsciously tried to convince myself I'm not 'that bad'; these people (whoever these people are) are worse. I thought of myself as no longer the liability one potential employer claimed I was during a call where he had to deliver the news about not being able to offer me a job—I am a productive member of society. And this, all of it, in all its...idiocy, was manifesting itself in how I now carried myself! *Ugh.* I've been overcompensating. I have become a walking, talking, spokesman for the notion that appearance is the first line of defense from judgement, and if you're agreeable and accommodating, the world wouldn't fear your 'blackness,' and I just realized it. The cushions solidified and became uncomfortable beneath my butt. Sweat congregated at the top of each brow. *I should go.*

A young man, obviously tired from working out, emerged from the hallway just right of the gym, headed toward the front door, donning a hoodie before braving the cold. *Why can't we just be cold? Yuck!* What a demoralizing realization, to know your hoodie could drum up suspicion, and potentially lead to the extinguishing of your life.

Sitting here in the foyer of my alma mater, in suit and tie, waiting to be interviewed about who I have become since graduating from the University of West Georgia...it's weird. 'They' think I was a productive citizen when I was here. I led a double life, however.

"Ummm? You're curious about me being here?"

"Absolutely. Your presence piqued my interest. Piqued is a great word. You used to host that TV show *Free Verse.* They still play it around here from time to time. I love that show. You wrote a couple of books too, right?"

"Yeah," I answered, now staring at this chubby-faced individual who seemed to know more about me than his quote suggested. "What's your name?"

"Charles. Forgive me if I'm being awkward. Socializing has never been a strength of mine."

"You're fine."

"You mind if I ask you a couple more questions?"

"Does that question count as one of the 'couple', Charles?" I replied. Again, I looked at my watch.

I hadn't expected an interview before the interview, but the exchange with Charles had a calming effect on my anxiety. I don't know at what point my mission directive shifted, but it did. My mind set on civilizing this man. Unbeknownst to me, I was trying to convince him to see the civility in me.

"What brought you to West Georgia?"

"Several reasons actually. It was one of three schools I got accepted to; I knew some folks who were down here already; it was far enough away from the city, and I needed the change in scenery."

"Why? Why did you need a change? Were you running from something?"

"What kind of question is that?"

"I don't know. I'm just curious. Most people who need a 'change in scenery' are running from something."

"Excuse me for a moment." I stood, buttoned my suit jacket, and went over to the receptionist, who was now cheerfully chatting on her cell phone, to inquire about how much longer it would be.

"Do you know how much longer?"

"He should be finished any minute."

"Okay," I said returning to my seat.

Chapter Nine
Issues with the universe

C harles had finished his water, and as I walked back, he waited for me to look at him before he shot the empty bottle into a nearby trash can. It went in. He also left his hand in the air, posing briefly before bringing it down and kissing his fingertips signifying his skill in garbage disposal.

"So... what were you running from?"

"Some guys were trying to kill me," I responded. There were various magazines on the coffee table just to the left of where we were sitting. I grabbed one as I sat down and began to thumb through it.

"You're kidding," Charles gulped, scooting to the edge of the divan.

"Nope."

"So, what happened? You must tell me the story, man. Don't leave me hanging!"

"Charles, I don't know if I'll have enough time. Mr. Daniels will be free any second, and I would hate to have to leave in the middle of the story."

"Awww man, don't worry about that! If it happens, it happens. Just tell me while we have some time to kill. No pun intended."

"Alright. I played baseball in high school."

"What position?"

"Third. I had been on varsity since tenth grade, one of my proudest achievements by the way, and we played year-round: fall ball, summer ball, winter ball, etc. I'd had an exceptional winter season and I eagerly looked forward to Spring. Our coach, Ron Elgin, who had coached at Lithonia for a long time prior to my senior year, quit right before the school year started. He abandoned us, left and went to Shiloh High in the burbs. A lot of my teammates saw this as a slap in the face because of the timing and the fact that he left us for a team that was predominantly white. Me, on the other hand, I worried about getting to know a new coach, you know? Our team had been playing together for a while and we all knew what role we played in the old system. As expected, the new coach came in with a new system and changed everything."

"I bet that had to suck."

"Yeah, it did. But we were up to the challenge and Shiloh was on our schedule—we'd show him. He didn't know it, but he had lit a fire in us. We were to beat his new team and shame him for abandoning us like that. Unfortunately, it didn't work out that way though."

"What happened?"

"Man, the day of, the universe conspired against us the entire day. Two of our best players got sick, and the bus never showed up to take us to the game. Luckily, we had eleven seniors on the team, so we car pooled. That was a mistake."

"Why? What happened?" Charles leaned in. He was clearly either a baseball fan or fond of train wrecks.

"Well, it was a good game," I said glancing over at the receptionist. "We traded runs, and in the bottom of the final inning, we had one out. We had runners on second and third, and the score was 4-3. There was a sacrifice fly to center field, the tying run scored, and the runner on second advanced to third. But, in 'good ole boy' fashion, Coach Elgin appealed. He claimed the runner on second left the base too early. The umpire agreed, resulting in a double-play. Game over."

"Wow."

"We were devastated. A couple of people cried, and others were angry. I was furious. I rode to the game with our catcher, Dontavious, and he and I left without shaking hands. We just bounced."

"That's not very sportsman-like, Estrell."

"You want me to finish this story, Charles? Watch it," I snapped. I placed the magazine I had picked up earlier on the couch between us and looked at the door to Mr. Daniels's office.

"Ouch. This is still a touchy subject for you, huh? I'm sorry. Proceed. Please."

"We raced back to school in silence. We had to be going at least 70 mph the whole way. We made it back to campus just before 7:00 pm as the sun was starting to set. We were first back, and the parking lot was all but vacant. There were two cars sitting at the far end of the lot; a blue Trailblazer and black Cavalier. They parked so the driver side windows were facing each other, and they appeared to be talking. We recognized the Cavalier. It belonged to a guy who was on the JV squad. They'd had a game that night as well. After a couple of minutes, the Cavalier came and parked beside us. The two younger teammates of ours, Tez and Eric, clearly upset, claimed the guys in the Trailblazer were from Rockbridge High School and were 'talking shit.' As they spoke, I looked over at the small SUV and watched it crawl from our parking lot with two of the four occupants hanging out the windows, giving us the finger."

"Jeez. They had some balls on them, huh?"

"Like I said. The universe conspired against us the whole day."

"It did! So, what happened next?"

Chapter Ten
Grace and Redemption

C harles scooted over. At this point, he was uncomfortably close to me.

"Ummm…" His proximity made me nervous. It felt like I could feel his breath on my face. *Where is Mr. Daniels!?!* "Ummm…I looked over at Dontavious. His eyes met mine, and we were on the same page. 'Let's get em.' The Trailblazer took off down the street, and we gave chase. Four of us and four of them—a decent party; that's what we called fights, just in case you were wondering."

"Duly noted."

"We followed them about a mile and a half before they turned into a neighborhood off York Road. The guys hopped out of their car and ran into a house in the middle of the block. We rode by the house, and turned around using a driveway about five or six houses down from the one they went into. We assumed they'd had a change of heart, and we were just going to go back to the school. We still had our baseball uniforms on and everything. As we started back down, multiple guys began to spill out into the street blocking our exit. That's when the shooting began. I thought we were going to die. Dontavious threw the car in reverse, and we sped, backwards, until we lost sight of the pack. Then we turned around and tried to find another way out. At some point, we lost the Cavalier, and we panicked. I was so scared. The neighborhood was one big U, so we didn't know whether they had circled back around and ran into those guys, if they'd been shot, held at gun point, nothing. Dontavious just kept saying, 'Damn, damn, damn. I knew we shouldn't have followed them, man.' "

"This is crazy, man!"

"Dontavious knew where Tez lived, so we went by his house to see if they were safe, but they weren't there. On the way back to the school, Tez called me and told us to meet him at his cousin's house. I tried to ask him what happened to them, but he quickly hung up. When we pulled up, there were four other cars, excluding the Cavalier, in the cul-de-sac, and a few guys were loading into them. Tez yelled for us to follow. We rode in a procession, car after car, and found our way back to the neighborhood where we last encountered the guys. This time we used the other entrance. We parked on the crest of the U, around the corner and out of sight. As we walked up the hill to get a look down the street toward their house, I asked Tez, 'What are we about to do?'

"He responded, 'We're about to get back at them.' "

"'That's when I noticed a couple of the guys who were with us were carrying guns. We stopped at the top of the hill. The boys who had shot at us earlier were all still standing outside. You could hear music. They were celebrating. I looked back over at Tez. He was putting his fingers in his ears.

My heart sank. Everything was happening in slow motion. The guys with guns raised their arms. I remember looking down toward the crowd, horrified. The first shot rang out. *Boom.* Then a second. *Boom.* The crowd dispersed in all directions, and the gunman kept firing. A body fell lifeless to the pavement."

"You saw someone get shot!?"

"I could tell by the way his body collapsed he wasn't diving out of the way."

"Oh, wow."

"It was one of the worst days of my life, Charles."

"Did you know the shooters?"

"No."

"What happened to the guy who got shot? Did he die?"

"When we got back in the car my cell phone was ringing. An old classmate who had transferred to Rockbridge a few years prior called and said those were his friends, and asked if we could chill out. I remembered him. He was a good dude."

"You can't be serious."

"I told him to call them and make sure all of them were okay and to call me back. He called about ten minutes later while I was in the locker room, and said that one of his friends was shot in the head. He had died on the way to the hospital. He was eighteen. He had a daughter. He was a good kid with his whole life in front of him. I will carry the weight of that with me for the rest of my days."

"You blame yourself for his death?"

"I take responsibility for the part I played in the events of that day. And that situation is why I am so sensitive to how precious life is."

"That situation changed your life, huh?

"Very much so."

"So, that's why you chose to come here? People were trying to retaliate?"

"Yeah. People would call the radio station and make threats. They knew our uniform numbers. People shot up our homes, shot up our parties, people got jumped on at the mall for wear school paraphernalia. This un-fortunate incident sparked one of the most intense school rivalries of our time."

"Did the police ever find the shooters?"

The door to Mr. Daniels's office opened, and a young lady walked out turning off the light behind her. I looked at the desk where the receptionist sat, and it was now vacant. While I was talking, the entire building had cleared out, and it was just Charles and me.

"What did the loss of that young man do to you?"

"You know, it took a very long time to get over it. It still bothers me today. Our choices, even the smallest ones, can define a lifetime."

"Pain and suffering are always inevitable for a large intelligence and a deep heart. The really great men must, I think, have great sadness on Earth."

"Another Dostoevsky quote?"

"You got it. Listen, I don't want to hold you up too long. I just have a few more questions since we're here."

"Okay."

"It doesn't seem like you're running anymore. Why come back now?"

"You want me to be honest?"

"Absolutely."

"When I was a kid, my peers used to make fun of me because I liked poetry. I just didn't know how to use it. This place, where I found and lost love more times than I care to recall, is where my love for words fell into place like a piece of jigsaw. I needed the cathartic release. I had so much to say. Here, my talent and passions manifested themselves, and I was applauded for it. I found my voice here. I just didn't know what I could and couldn't say once I left. Does that make sense?"

"It does."

"Speech isn't free, sir."

"Agreed."

"Look, Socratic thinking is the single greatest thing I learned in college, but there wasn't a lot of delving into the deep recesses of my mind because I didn't want to fail. College wasn't a time for lofty exploration of thought and deconstructing ideas. It was four years of figuring out how not to go back to my father's house. There was a bunch of grappling, and not knowing how to respond to what the world had to offer me. All I knew was physical violence and anger. But you can't punch everybody. You can't fight every battle. You can't civilize everyone. So now the question is 'How can I help?' "

"Help who? Is this why you're a Public Defender?"

"Charles, there are a lot of underrepresented populations: minorities, addicts, felons, the poor. Bryan Stevenson said, 'God's people have been called to be proximate to those who have fallen down, the suffering.' For a long time, I did my job from the perspective of atonement for the transgressions of my past. Things I saw here contributed to me losing sight of who I am. But I got a second chance. I now understand the power of grace and redemption. By God's grace, the metric system for which I measure myself is different from the one the world uses. I am more than the color of my skin, and I am more than the worst thing I've ever done. That's a message no one ever told me. That's what I came back to say. That's the good news."

"Okay. I like it, Estrell. So, what's next?"

"I don't know, Mr. Daniels. Maybe kayaking."

Baptism

Chapter Eleven
Seasoning

March 12, 2016

The day was unseasonably warm. Seventy-seven degrees, with a nice breeze, and ocean-blue sky peeking through cumulus clouds. The night prior, my best friend, Casey, suggested we go kayaking on the Yellow River after I had got off work. I jumped at the chance. Let me tell it, I am an outdoorsman, but during my childhood such opportunities often eluded me. That morning I walked into work with every intention of getting in and out as quickly as possible. I taught an abbreviated version of a lesson on emotional manipulation to my adolescent audience, and left early to go home and change. I teach a course called WAIT, which is an acronym for Why Am I Tempted. It's about living and loving well with an emphasis on healthy relationships.

Anyway, I'd never been kayaking on a river. The idea was an intriguing one and I enjoyed spending time with the homie...so why not?

Casey and I go way back. Ours was an organic friendship whose origin derived from my time as an intern with the public defender's office in Covington, Georgia. I met Casey the day I interviewed for the position. He sat in while the boss and I discussed my lack of qualifications and the gaping hole in my resume. I remember feeling like Nathaniel Ayers in *The Soloist*, and I asked them to pardon my resume's appearance because I'd had a few setbacks. I also said to them, "As a semi-ex-criminal turned college grad, life hasn't been no 'crystal stair,' and the only way for me to pay my penance was to be of service." Casey called

BS and we all had a good laugh. For some reason, they gave me the gig and, over time, he became one of my closest friends.

We were an odd couple of dudes in that we had nothing in common. He is a white country boy from the backwoods of Georgia, and I am Black, just a gunshot wound away from embodying all the thuggish platitudes that come from the hood. He is simple, slow to anger, and good with money. I am sort of outgoing, immature, and handsome. I secretly wanted to be like him. Commonly, awkward social situations made us anxious; we both had odd senses of humor, and we possessed varying degrees of thoughtfulness. It is my belief that these things solidified this camaraderie.

From the beginning, intentional or not, it was like the re-education of a Negro. He introduced me to absurdities I had never considered like mud'n, noddle'n, and bonfires in the middle of nowhere. For those experiences, I am forever grateful. Some of that stuff was fun. Conversely, I taught him how to rock a suit and how to season…everything. We spoke at great length about the difference between sew-ins and lace fronts, because the idea of weave fascinated him. Growing up with a houseful of women allowed me to learn this firsthand. I gladly schooled my brother from another mother.

You see, I have always found that the beauty of life is in seeing everyone as similar. We are all human beings. Once you recognize that, view each other through a lens of commonality and set them as a baseline, everything else is seasoning. And I love seasoning.

Over the years, our friendship had matured. Casey got married. His wife, Brittany, rewrote our script, and virtually shut fun down as we knew it! There were no more late nights at the bar, wild weekend trips to Vegas, or lunch with the fellas. His priorities were different. He was now a husband and doing the family thing; hard.

I, on the other hand, had taken a new job a couple of counties away. I was living the single life; I was out here thot'n and plot'n, so it made sense for Brittany to pump the brakes on the amount of time I spent with him when she did. If I could insert a sad emoji here, I would. I missed my friend.

Consequently, the time we did spend together was different, weightier, especially after Brittany got pregnant. Life was no longer a thing spoken about in the abstract. Casey would be a father, and when baby Emmy finally entered this world, I completely understood why I saw Casey less and less.

I was elated when he called unexpectedly and invited me kayaking. Yeah, kayaking. It would be disingenuous of me to say I had ever thought about traversing a river in a little old boat but, after considering all the pros and cons, I decided some time is better than none.

Chapter Twelve
Rinky-dink what?

I arrived at his house around 2:30 p.m. He was already outside loading the truck. He smiled and waved. Casey stands about 5'7" and his torso is approximately the same length as his legs. He was a stocky little fellow, sporting a red Outdoor Originals T-shirt, black swimming trunks, and a specially made size 8½ Atlanta Braves ball cap that covered his short brown hair. Yes, my friend is built like a bobblehead of a minor-league second baseman.

"What's up, my man?" he asked, as he greeted me with our signature double-tap handshake.

"This is! I'm pretty excited." I could feel the brown paper bag I was carrying partially tear from the grip of my sweaty palms. "You want to take a shot first?" I was nervous. It was going to take more than the Mangoritas Casey requested I bring to calm my nerves. For that trick, I bought three small bottles of Crown, one of which I had already downed before I got out of the car.

"Hell yeah," he replied closing the tailgate with a solid thump.

I passed him a bottle hoping he hadn't been drinking already. I needed him sober. I said a little prayer to myself asking God for an uneventful trip.

"I'm glad one of us has done this before. I was up all-night thinking about it. You know black people, except for Simone Manuel, typically aren't good at water sports," I said showing him a picture on my cell phone of her in all of her glory. "Black women rock."

"Yeah, man. I think I remember reading something about that on Wikipedia. I have to warn you—" I looked up from my phone. Casey's head tilted slightly to the right, and a smirk was dangling from the corner of his lips. "The place we're launching from is sketchy. It's right off the road, under a bridge, and behind a rinky-dink trailer park. But once we're in the water it'll be smooth sailing."

"Under a bridge and behind a rinky-dink what?" The last time he had to give me a disclaimer about a place we were going, I ended up in the deep backwoods of Oxford surrounded by rednecks drinking beer, listening to Lynyrd Skynyrd, and burning stuff. It had turned out to be surprisingly fun. "Why did you wait until the last minute to mention this?"

"Because I don't want to hear your mouth when we pull up and you see it. You know how you get when things look…suspect."

I had to laugh. He knew me well. And I was no stranger to adjusting and rolling with the flow of things. I did not have a problem ducking or running when things went left. Coming from where I came from, you needed to be crafty. We both knew his survival chances were a whole lot better than mine in these types of situations. I was faster, but he was white.

"Whatever, man. So, what's the plan?" I said.

"We're going down the river, son! We can do a little fishing, sip on suds, and relax. It's going to be real peaceful," Casey answered as he opened the bottle of Crown I brought him and raised it in the air.

"I'm down with that, but what are the conditions like? You know I don't have a ton of experience with kayaking. I kayaked in the ocean atop scary but calm waters. I ain't trying to be rolling through no rapids, juggling beer and fishing gear. Furthermore, I am not interested in drowning. Do you know how embarrassing it would be to be the Yellow River's first black victim?" I cracked the seal of my bottle and tapped it against his.

"Ninja, please. I am not taking you through any rapids. Your momma ain't about to kill me! Plus, this is one of the slower-moving rivers. That's why I picked it."

Now, in case you're wondering, Casey and I have discussed my thoughts and feelings about the use of the n-word by white people, and have concluded that, among friends and never in public, he could use the non-pejorative word "ninja" in the place of the other racial epithet that begins with the letter "n." Moving on.

We both chuckled and toasted. We drank to our adventure and our friendship. The Crown went to work at once. It warmed my chest and took the edge off. Casey's cheeks had taken on a rosy tint, indicating he felt it too. He began to load the Mangoritas in a cooler he had gotten from the garage and covered them with ice.

"Yo, why did you want those?" I asked pointing to the little silver-and-mango-colored cans because I had never seen a guy drink one. Even the clerk at the store inquired as to whether or not I was trying to "get lucky" tonight by purchasing the 24-pack."

"Bro, haven't you heard? This shit is refreshing." Casey held up one of the cans and grinned like a Cheshire cat. He should've been in the commercial.

"I can't believe you still enjoy those girly drinks! For the life of me, I just don't understand."

While I continued to ridicule Casey about his beverage of choice, Brittany walked out of the house with a sleeping Emmy in her arms. Brittany carefully passed her to Casey, and he loaded her into the car seat in the cab of his truck.

"Let's roll," she whispered, opening the driver's side door and hopping in.

I grabbed my bag from the bench near the door, and switched out of my tennis shoes into some clogs Casey was kind enough to lend me. I forgot my water shoes at home.

"Damn rookie."

I gave him the finger and helped him get the rest of the gear into the truck. Then we took off.

* * *

The booming sound of Casey's engine radiating from his new exhaust pipes offered a drum line to the relatively quiet ride. I was silently freaking out beside Emmy and was trying to focus on my breathing to slow my heart rate. I looked out the window. The sprawling grasslands of the country with its rolling hills and endless greenery gave me a fair amount of peace, until I noticed all the washed-out Georgia clay seeping onto the roadway. We had received a lot of rain recently, and today was the first full day of sunshine in two weeks. It suddenly occurred to me that river conditions might not be so typical after all.

"Yo, I think the water levels are going to be pretty high, man. When I was fishing at your dad's house with my mom this weekend, it was back up to the garden gnome. I can't remember the last time it was that high, and we've had much more rain since," I said, still looking out the window. As far as I was concerned, it wasn't too late to turn around, but I didn't want to be the person who pulled the plug.

"It's cool. Water levels don't matter when you're in a boat." Brittany joined him in a simultaneous chuckle. My idea of subtly suggesting we reconsider evaporated while they laughed at me. *Damn.*

"The only thing we need to pay attention to is the current. It normally takes three hours to travel the river," he said looking at his watch. "So, Brittany will pick us up around six. If the current is fast, we'll just need to give her a call early."

"I'm glad you've done this before. Did I mention that already? I want to be clear. If you hadn't…I'd be nervous."

Casey spun around in his seat. His eyes were small and piercing. He knew.

"Who do you think you're fooling, Estrell? We know you're nervous."

We exited the highway at Almon Road. When the light changed, Brittany moved forward entering the turning lane and made a left onto the Access Road. She slowed down. Sketchy was right!

"We're almost there!" she exclaimed in jubilant fashion. For someone who wasn't going with us, Brittany appeared to be excited and really invested in our little adventure. I began to panic. My imagination tried to run away with me; I thought about leeches, flesh-eating parasites, and the young girl who lost all her limbs after taking a fall in a river a couple of years ago.

"Brittany, what are you and Emmy going to do today?" I queried while still trying to calm my nerves. She practically glared at me through the rearview as if I had just revealed the secret she had been keeping about a surprise birthday party or something. I intentionally looked away. I looked over at Emmy. She was still sound asleep in her car seat next to me. I smiled as I watched as her little head bobbed from side to side. This offered a momentary distraction.

We're going to get our nails done and do a little shopping, Estrell."

"We're here!" Casey proclaimed with the timing of Columbus.

We turned onto a small gravel road off to the right which folded back onto itself and disappeared over a ridge. The area was decorated by burnt-out trailers and lawn chairs strewn about; there was an old rusty tricycle, and a tire swing, the rope of which looked like it was on its last strand.

"What kind of shit is this?" I said not expecting any kind of response.

"Man, stop crying. I already told you this area looked sketchy, but it really wasn't. The meth houses have been boarded up, and the cats that ran them are either in jail or dead. Our problem is we can't get the truck to the bank because of those three green bollards." Casey pointed to the stocky poles protruding from the ground. "We're going to have to carry the kayaks to the river. Man up." He unbuckled his seatbelt as his wife brought the truck to a stop.

I slid up in my seat, right next to Casey, inches from his ear, and outside the hearing range of his beautiful baby girl, and whispered a long, drawn, "F*#! youuuuuuu." *Bring it!*

Brittany got out of the truck first. "I'm going to go look at the river." I watched her until she disappeared over the hill. I disembarked next. I decided I should stretch because we were going to be sitting in small boats for the next three hours. There's nothing like catching a cramp in your thigh when you're confined to a tight space.

"Grab this end," Casey said as he carefully released the tailgate and slid his kayak toward him.

"I'll be right with you, my man," I grunted as I rose from my toe touches. Brittany reappeared.

"It's beautiful down there, you guys. The water is moving pretty fast though."

Casey and I placed both kayaks on the ground. At first, we tried to carry them at the same time, but it didn't work.

"That's cool," Casey replied to Brittany. "Be expecting a call earlier if it's really fast."

"Will do."

She got back in the truck and put it in gear. She rolled the window down and kissed Casey goodbye. "You take care of my husband, Estrell. I don't want to have to hurt you," she said to me as she pulled off leaving us in a cloud of orange dust.

Chapter Thirteen
The Water/Fish'n

Here. Let's put your boat in first so I can help you push off," Casey suggested as he scooted my olive-green kayak toward the water.

The bank was rocky with stones the size of couch cushions. Rocks closer to the water's edge formed natural steps where the water had previously whitewashed the area. I climbed in the boat and shoved away from the rocks using the oar. I could feel the power of the water immediately. If I closed my eyes, you couldn't tell me I wasn't in a Jacuzzi, but it wasn't that comfortable. Baby, it was cold! The strength of the current moved us. It was as if we'd gotten on a treadmill at full speed. If I wanted to stay upright, I'd need to adjust before I let go of the handrail, lest my feet fly out from beneath me. It was overwhelming at first, being in the hands of Mother Nature's raw power. I finagled a way to slow myself in order not to leave Casey. And I could not leave Casey. To complicate things the water near the bank was shallow, which made it tough to paddle.

"Hurry up!" I pleaded in a serious but joking manner.

Casey had one foot in the water and the other foot in the boat. This wasn't his first rodeo. He was in total control. In one swift move, he pushed off the bank and was in the water, smoother than! He paddled past me, and we began to coast downstream.

The river was beautiful, a chocolate-milk-brown-and-reddish-mixed tributary clawing its way through the backyards of country folk. The water was murky. Visibility was limited to just above the surface but it wasn't spooky.

"Man, it's beautiful out here," I marveled.

Casey reached into his tackle box and grabbed his lure; a little plastic green lizard about the size of one you'd find in your garden. He fastened it to the hook, picked up the rod, and looked at me.

"Hey man, you want to do some fishing?"

"Let me see you do it first." Novice that I was, I wasn't sure about trying too many new things at once. The goal was to remain in the boat the whole time; everything else would be extra.

I orientated my boat so I could observe his technique and ensure I was out of the way of his flying tackle. Casey turned his boat around so that he was floating down the river backward.

"Set yourself up like this so when you cast, the current will do all the work."

With a flick of his wrist, the lizard kissed the ochre bank and dropped into the water. Sweet! He made it look so easy. Casey reeled in his artificial bait, and repeated this exercise a couple of times before I mustered up enough courage to try it.

"I got this. Hand it here, playa," I requested eagerly with my arm outstretched. Casey paddled over to me, positioning his kayak next to mine. He passed me the rod and resituated the lure for me. Then he reached into the cooler and retrieved two ice-cold Mangoritas, handing one to me. We whacked cans, Viking-style, sloshing suds upon our wrists and drank.

"Happy hunting, my brother," Casey offered, pushing off, giving me room to maneuver. He smiled like a proud poppa as he watched me. Like an apprentice under the tutelage of his instructor, I mimicked his every move; I rotated my vessel one-hundred-and-eighty degrees, and gently kissed the lizard off the riverbank. Unfortunately, my bait didn't fall into the water. It decided to ricochet its small, lifeless, poor excuse for a body, off the clay and entangle itself in some brush. It was an epic fail. Casey had to go in and save that damn lizard.

"Happens to the best of us," he yakked as he emancipated it.

"Uh huh. Just get me back in business, bro. I'm gonna catch the first fish."

"There you go."

I summoned the bait back to my boat, resituated it on the hook, and prepared it for immediate relaunch. This time, I waited until the coast was clear and executed an out-standing 9.5 out of 10 on the landing, with bank-kiss included. Plunk! The small splash pleased me greatly. As I began to reel out of the Cimmerian depths, a glint of silver caught my eye and sprinted beneath the surface toward my unassuming lizard. Strike!

"I got one!" I shouted almost tipping the boat in my enthusiasm.

"Yeah, you do!" Casey clapped with excitement.

The tip of my rod bent and arced with little regard for its own constitution. The silver zigzagged and danced like the sun across the top of the water. I spun the reel urgently to land the fish before it darted into a crevasse or under a sunken tree or something.

"Keep it tight, man! You got this!" Casey cheered.

All of my attention was focused on that fish, when I felt the slap, scratch, and scraping from branches of a tree that I, myself, had run into while navigating this river backward.

"Damn, homie. Are you okay?" There was merriment in Casey's eyes and laughter in his voice. It was a foregone conclusion I would be the butt of multiple jokes by the end of the day.

"Yeah, I'm good," I replied as I fought my way out the other side. During the struggle, I held the rod down, almost in the water, so the line would not get caught up. Through it all, I was able to land the beast once free from the tentacles of that fallen timber.

"Wow. Would you look at that?!"

* * *

The beast, a massive...half a pound of multi-colored pure freshness. Its body sparkled silver and chartreuse, and its belly glinted the most radiant color of red. I thought it was a piranha. With my left hand, I took hold of the fish. I secured it in my palm and excised the hook with my right. I then held it up by its bottom lip for Casey to take in all its glory.

"Ain't she a beaut?" I gloated.

"She certainly is. Are you going to keep her?"

"Nah," I said, tossing my catch back into the brown fog. What kind of question was that? Where was I going to put a fish? The thought of it flopping around in the boat made me cringe. "Are you going to keep it?" I scoffed to myself.

Over the next thirty or so minutes, I fished, on and off, experimenting with different styles of casting, and retrieving the lizard. Like a puppeteer to the lure, I tried everything: jigging, hopping, twitching, and jerking to see if I was as good of an angler as I was in my head. Unluckily, I didn't catch anything else, not one bite, but life was good. I reeled in one last time, placed the rod down, and reoriented my boat forward. I sat back, nestled my butt into a more comfortable position with the oar across my lap, and exhaled.

Who would've thought it would turn out like this? Everything had come together in perfect harmony and culminated in this moment. Who would've thunk it? Certainly not me. I'm creative, but my imagination was not that good. Someone else was pushing this pen which orchestrated my life. I was beginning to believe the author had taken a liking to me. Times like this made me think of my grandpa. He would've enjoyed this. It was perfect.

"Hey man, do you remember your first day as an intern with us?" Casey asked pulling even with me. We paddled in unison to navigate some trees down in the river.

"Oh shit…" I hit one with the side of my kayak, and it turned me sideways where I was skidding down it, similar to the way skateboarders glide down rails. Fortunately, I managed to correct my vessel once it disengaged. *Whew.* Scary, but it wasn't a big deal.

"You mean the day you guys changed my life? I sure do."

"Was it that serious?"

"Absolutely. At the time, I had nothing going for me except that court case I was fighting. I was living back at home with my father. I was broke and spending every penny I came across at local bars. It was a dark time. I remember it like it was yesterday."

"That's deep. How did you hear about the position?"

"Well, my father's landlord is a Superior Court judge, and I guess he told him I graduated and didn't know what I was going to do for a career. The judge gave my dad a card with the contact information of the Public Defender's Office written on it, and he slid it under my door one morning. Man, the memory is so vivid. It was a Friday, and I had slept in because I was out drinking into the wee hours of the morning. Dad knocked and said, 'Hey bud, give these folks a call when you get a chance.' At first, it kind of made me mad, because once he woke me up, I couldn't go back to sleep. Eventually, I just got up, grabbed the card and my cell. While sitting on the edge of my bed, in a wifebeater and boxers, I made the call. Anthony answered the phone…"

The river widened, and the terrain on each side changed from trees and dense foliage to backyards and open air. Just ahead, you could see a snake swimming atop the water, and I made small strokes with the oar to give him as much room as he needed.

"Anthony answered the phone, and I told him I was interested in the intern position. He told me how he had received a little information about me from the judge. He asked me what I was doing that morning and if I could come by for an interview.

There I was, edge of my bed, head spinning, and looking a hot mess, but I had nothing to lose. I threw some clothes on and came on over. The best decision I've ever made."

"You didn't even shower first? That's just nasty, Estrell."

"Bite me, Casey."

"Hell naw! Who knows if you've showered today?" Casey said making his way over to me and handing me another Mangorita.

"Whatever. I still have that card too. Maybe I should frame it or something," I said snapping open my can and taking a sip.

"You should. You have an exceptional story to go with it and everything. Your walking through our doors was the second-best thing that happened to that office. First being my arrival, of course."

"I hear ya. Now it just feels like things are too good to be true. When I walked through those doors all those years ago, there was a gray cloud over my head, and it followed me everywhere. I couldn't shake it. But then, my clouds parted, revealing the Sun, gradually. Remember? I went from making $0/week to $200 in the blink of an eye. You helped me pay off my debts; I bought a house, and then Samantha."

"Samantha? Who is that? Sounds like a European prostitute."

"Samantha is my car, fool. The Infiniti."

"Ahhhhhhh. You never know with you, kiddo. It is a nice car though. So, what are you griping about? Are you afraid of losing it all?"

"Yeah. I'm afraid of ruining it. Or something happening that would jeopardize it all. I mean, you never know what you don't know, and that's how the world gets you. You think you have all the bases covered and then...bam." I slapped the oar on the water to drive home my point.

"That makes sense." How's the love life going?"

I looked at Casey. "Dang, that was an interesting transition falling a couple inches short of random."

Casey chuckled. "I'm sorry, man. It's just that no one knows what tomorrow will bring. You will never have enough money; your job will never be totally secure, and hell; the wind might even carry your woman to another man's bed. At the end of the day, we're all just out here."

"Well, since you put it that way...I've put the love life on hold," I said

"What? What happened to ole girl? I thought you guys hit it off famously. You talked so highly of her."

Chapter Fourteen

See what had happened was...

We approached a bend in the river that took the shape of an elbow. Here the current picked up the pace, and boulders created whitecaps and small rapids. Casey and I split up to take advantage of mildly exhilarating crests on each side.

"The trick to these is not to let the front of your boat hit the rapid head-on. Try to hit it at an angle, if you can."

"What happens if you hit the rapid head-on? I mean, worst-case scenario." I wasn't trying to invite trouble. I just wanted to know.

"You go for a little swim, my friend."

I began to paddle swiftly to pick up some speed. Imagine a professional BMX rider going into a jump…well, that's certainly not me heading into this rapid. I steered my craft to the right and put the tip of the oar in the water which angled the boat. There was a dip and a splash, and it was over. Calm was restored to the water, and we moved on.

"Soooooooo?" Casey started, knowing I hadn't forgotten the last question he had posed to me.

"It's over, man. What can I say?"

"You can tell me what happened."

"She didn't want anything serious. Or, at least not with me. She had a ton of excuses but, at the end of the day, she said that when we met, 'we were too available.' I've concluded that that's because she prefers men who aren't…available."

"But she still wanted to be a part of your life, right? She wanted to be friends with benefits, basically?"

"Yeah. And I have enough friends, man. If I were trying to still be out here thot'n and plot'n, I would. I'm tired of that. Casual, meaningless sex isn't all that it's cracked up to be. I would like to build something with someone like what you have with your wife. I want a woman to come in and shut fun down!"

"So, it's just over? You're not going to talk to her anymore? You just packed up shop and left town?"

"Yeah. I look at it like this; if you don't want me, leave me alone. I'm not about to be blocking my blessings by sitting around and trying to convince some woman I'm worth the leap. That's for the birds. Plus, Valerie asked me a question that really blew my mind; I mean, a real 'mind-f*cker.'"

"Who is Valerie?"

"Valerie is a social worker in my office, and she's a licensed therapist. I run things by her every time I think I'm trip'n."

"Okay...what did she ask you?"

"She asked me if I thought ole girl was selfish because she didn't want to spend the rest of her life with me. And she asked me if I was doing everything I was doing to convince her to."

"You told Valerie she was selfish? That's deep."

"Tell me about it! I spent a whole week trying to reconcile my actions and figuring out whether I was doing all this to obtain ole girl's heart. Then, once I came to a conclusion, I had to ask myself if I actually wanted it. It's like those women who say you must wait a certain period of time before you guys have sex knowing damn well we can wait. That turns into a game. We ignore all the red flags that void your credentials as relationship material until we smash. Then we're straight. You can keep that. I don't want to be that guy anymore walking around with a jar full of hearts."

"That's good, homie. I'm glad you got out before one of y'all got hurt. What's next?"

"Good question. I'm just going to focus on myself for a while. I need to get my finances in order and lose some of this weight."

"What's wrong with your paper?"

"What's right? I'm single. I should have no credit card debt and at least 10k in the bank."

"I thought we got your affairs back in order...what happened?"

"See, what had happened was…" I began to scratch my head like men do when they don't have a real excuse for what they've done, just something they came up with to get the spotlight off themselves, "…I've been out here trick'n off. I've been living above my means. It's been keeping me up at night."

"Is that right?"

"Yep. Now I'm going to get my money right for when Ms. Right does come along."

* * *

Looking forward, Casey called out, "Hey man, you have another tree coming up on you."

What appeared to be a thick branch, about the width of a wooden bat but much longer, was ahead of me swaying with the current. I had taken my eye off the prize (staying in the boat) and allowed my feelings to take me completely out of the present. For a second, I panicked, but I willed myself to slow down and think. I submerged the oar in the water off the right side of the boat, angling it. The front began to turn clockwise setting us up for a glancing blow. The pace of the turn was too fast though. Smack! The kayak and I hit said branch with a solid, sideways, collision. At first, the timber gave with the force of the blow, and I thought I was just going to break right through it. This was not the case. The branch absorbed the contact and stood its ground, pinning the side of my vessel to it. Instinctively, I began to paddle on the opposite side to keep the boat upright. This action worked for a moment and gave me an opportunity to assess the situation. Casey had turned his kayak and was cautiously paddling toward me.

"What should I do?" I asked nervously while still managing to paddle and keep the boat up.

"Paddle on the right side!"

Now, you should note that at this point, Casey's perspective was different from mine because he was facing me. The current was flowing right to left bearing down on my left shoulder, and I was pinned horizontally to this immovable object on my right. So, when Casey suggested I paddle on the right side, one stroke of the oar was all that was needed to send me toppling over and leave me trapped, submerged underwater.

The chill from the river was paralyzing, but jarring enough to encourage movement. I drew a single, deep breath as I took the plunge, so even though I was underwater, upside down, and pinned to what I found to be a whole damn tree, I wasn't drowning. Time was of the essence, though. Every second counted.

Still holding my breath, I struggled to free myself from the very vessel which had, moments before, carried me down this estuary. It now appeared to be intent on keeping me hostage. I could wiggle the upper half of my body. My foot was wedged inside the boat. Casey's clogs were comfortably standing between me and freedom. *Oh, this is just great.* Making the decision to ditch the shoe was an easy one. I could buy Casey a new pair. I, on the other hand, was irreplaceable. I am exaggerating, but you get the point.

I swam out of the kayak and, upon my exit, my 200-pound frame met instantly with the wicked thrust of the current, trapping outside but under the boat. I thrashed and flailed trying to right myself. I desperately searched with my feet for the bottom but it was too deep. My body was flung, knocking the last bit of breath from my body and I was forced, again, to meet that same branch that had taken hold of my life and turned it on its head. *I can't breathe. Help!* All the complaints about not being where I wanted to be in life, and gripes about women, were expelled when that last bit of air escaped from my lips. I had to do something. *Where is Casey!?!*

The icy water seeped into my bones, and there was no other choice than to make a last-ditch effort to save myself. *I can't die like this.* My adrenaline was pumping. I maneuvered my body, gathering my feet and bracing them against the tree. The current tried relentlessly to keep me there, but pure resolve and a will to live empowered me to push off like an Olympic free-swimmer off the pool wall.

I took on a mouthful of water but this move propelled me away from that needy branch, and my out-flung arms grabbed the side of the boat. I pulled myself up. Only my head broke the surface and, with great urgency, though choking, I inhaled. *Air!*

The entire episode probably lasted twenty seconds, but it felt like forever. I gulped down as much relief as I could, but the current was pulling me back under the boat. My struggles weren't over. I wasn't in the clear yet. In the corner of my eye, I could see Casey paddling toward me.

"Hey man, are you alright? You scared the shit out of me. Can you stand up?"

Between gulps of air and spitting out water I managed to get out, "No."

"Well, can you swim to shore?"

"I think so." This response came out without a thought. My brain hadn't realized how much energy I had used up trying to live. My brain hadn't crunched the necessary numbers to complete such a task. You would've had to be a very strong swimmer, at the peak of your conditioning to swim against that current and to make it to the bank before the opportunity slipped away.

Unwisely, I let go of the side of the boat and tried to power swim the fifty or so yards to the clearing. I made it all of three full breaststrokes when it dawned on me that this wasn't a strength I owned. At least not at this moment. I should've said no. Despite my weakest effort, the water shoved me right past my small chance to exit and began to carry me, boat-less, downstream. I spun around to tell Casey I would meet him at the crossroads, trying to make light of the situation with a Bone Thugs-N-Harmony reference about dying, as it was the least I could do. But Casey was in trouble.

He had managed to collect all the scattered remnants of my shipwreck, in one arm, and was trying to save my kayak from sinking with the other. It belonged to a friend's father, so I can understand him not wanting to have to explain this when he showed up at their house empty-handed. But Casey was in trouble. The boat was dragging him down. With his right arm grossly hyper-extended, he toiled for dear life. His face was red with strain, and veins were popping out of everywhere.

"Yo, let the boat go! I'll catch it downstream," I yelled desperately.

"Urgh!" Casey exclaimed, turning the soon-to-be-submarine loose, and comporting himself to pursue both of us.

The temperature of the water was beginning to take its toll on my body. My muscles cramped and limbs stiffened, but that wasn't the worst of it. I was floating down a river with one shoe on, no ability to slow down or maneuver, and no means to defend myself against things unseen beneath the surface. I suffered minor bumps, bruises, scrapes, and cuts from who knows what, and I am fairly certain there was an '83 Volkswagen Beetle down there, just sitting. This was no walk in the park.

About a mile and a half from where this saga began, my feet pierced the sand and stopped my progress like an anchor. There, the depth was neck high, and as long as I could tolerate the waves slapping me in the face, I was safe. Or, at least that was the case before I turned around and saw my own kayak bearing down on me, like a car that has shifted out of park on a hill, and I was a kid standing behind it. *I'm going to have to stop it.* Once more, I cannot stress enough that my brain wasn't functioning at a level suitable to be making these types of decisions. I mean, this was an eight-foot boat, weighted down with water, torpedoing toward me, and powered by a force only matched by the hand of God. *This is going to be interesting.*

The closing speed of my now upside down, waterlogged, unmanned watercraft was quite impressive, and it is truly my belief that I would've lost my head had I not ducked seconds before impact. As the boat passed overhead, it afforded me a single opportunity to right it, so naturally, that's what I did. I crouched down in the freezing water, submerging myself, and sprung upward with both arms extended, punching the left side of the boat causing it to flip back over. The force of the blow unsettled my feet from the sand, and in order not to be left behind, I hitched a ride by holding onto its side. Casey paddled alongside.

"How you doing, brother?"

"I've seen better days. I busted up my leg pretty good, but I can't tell if it's bleeding and I'm afraid to look."

"Damn. I guess you lost your shades too, huh?"

"Sure did. This sucks, man."

"Yeah, this wasn't a part of the plan, and I could never really tell how dire the situation was. When you first went down, I thought it was funny, but when you went under the second time...I'm just glad you're alright."

* * *

Casey looked off into the distance, and I understood. We drifted down the river in silence for the next few minutes. Frigid and assertive water gave way to passive, chest-high current and, finally, I could take a break. My boat still had a couple of feet of water in its innards making it at least a couple of hundred pounds. Nevertheless, I tipped it over and drained most of it without a problem because it was time to go home. I steadied the kayak and tried, foolishly, to jump on top of it. I had convinced myself I could use it as a surfboard and ride it to safety. It began to sink again, immediately.

"Ummm...that's not going to work."

"You thought it would?"

"Shut up, Casey."

There was another tree lying in the water about ten yards from where we were so, again, I summoned some strength to drag the boat to it. I propped it against one of the limbs, turned it on its side, and drained it once more.

"You got any ideas?" I asked Casey, running on fumes.

"If my memory serves me correctly, we should be able to beach around this next bend. This stretch of the river is eight miles, and I want to say we've only completed a fourth."

"A fourth?!"

"Yeah, give or take. This little catastrophe may have taken forty-five minutes, but I'd say we've covered two miles."

I shoved off the tree and began to doggie paddle with my boat down the river, Casey in tow. I think he could tell I was upset, but we knew each other well enough to know this wasn't anyone's fault. Around the next bend, Casey's memory came through. There was a small beach of sand, and silt the color of red copper in front of dense woods. You could tell wildlife came here to drink by all the tracks coming and going. We beached our little boats and stretched. Shivering, I rang out my shirt and bucket hat, the only two things that stayed on me, and retrieved Casey's other clog from its bondage with a lighthearted chuckle. I looked at my watch. It was flashing all sorts of funky colors. The river had claimed it too.

"This has been one for the memory books," I said, putting the shoe on. "Hey, I'm not trying to hang around here too long. How fast do you think we can do these six miles?"

"That depends on how much energy you have left."

"Wipe that smirk off your face. Hand me two of those Mangoritas and let's bounce."

"Say no more."

We covered those six miles in a little under an hour. Casey called Brittany twenty minutes before we made it to the end, so she was pulling up just as we arrived. Emmy, awake from her nap, was first out of the truck and she ran down the shore to greet us.

"Hey, Daddy!"

"Hey, my little munchkin! What have you been doing today?"

"Mommy got my nails done," she said wiggling and showing off her multi-colored claws.

"Aww, that's cool!"

Brittany came down as we carried the boats, one by one, to the truck and loaded up.

"Estrell! What happened to you?"

"I got baptized."

In retrospect, I went to that river bogged down by life and I contributed greatly to the weight of the boat. My shoulders toted every single fear of failure and inadequacy, the self-sabotage and excuses, the addiction, and the crutches I had picked up over the years. That backpack was heavy and unrelenting. This baptism brought clarity to the muck and those vices that had handicapped and stifled my life, rendering my light dim, now lying on that riverbed along with my Ray-Bans. This is what I prayed for, and I'll never be the same.

Close Call

Chapter Fifteen
Pre-game'n

Rob pressed the tall, slender, 2oz shooter into the palm of my hand. It was cold. A condensation trickled down my forearm and we stood, standing shoulder to shoulder, around the island in the middle of my kitchen. We raised our glasses.

"A toast. Drink up, bruh. It's your birthday!"

"To not making the same mistakes twice and always striving to be better than we used to be!"

The curiously large shot of Patron went down with an ease I'm not particularly proud to say I have. A few drips spilled from the corner of my lips; the rest scorched my throat and warmed my belly.

"That's right, E…" Rob said placing his hand on my shoulder. "It's about to go down, homie. We're about to get chocolate wasted!" He had this silly-looking grin on his face.

"That's not how that saying goes."

"Man, I could care less! Why you always gotta be so proper? I'm about to party. I've been waiting on this night all week. Hell, I've been waiting on this night all year my brother." Rob poured himself another shot and downed it. He was getting to it a lot quicker than usual. *Something must be up.*

It was a warm October night, like many the world had strung together in recent years during seasons when it's supposed to be cold. We were all wearing either tees or polo's and jeans or chinos, bar hop'n attire.

"What's good, Rob? You look like you have something on your mind," I asked.

"It's nothing. I'm good."

"Uh huh."

"I just wish…" *Here we go.* "I just wish we could go back to the good old days. When all we had to worry about was booty and baseball…you know?"

I turned toward him to make sure I was following this new thread and slid my glass across the arctic-brown granite countertop for a refill.

"Yeah…I know. Before J-O-B-S and responsibilities became 'a real thing'. Back when the worst thing was getting caught outside when the streetlights came on or when your mom found your stash of condoms and said, 'we need to talk'."

"True."

"My thing was running out of minutes for my phone before I got all of the directions to where I was going. That was the worst!" Marlin offered. He had been in the bathroom for the last thirty minutes. He casually grabbed a shot glass from the cabinet and joined us. Marlin was Rob's cousin from Detroit, and he was in town on sabbatical from work. I think he got fired.

"Yeah, and before I had a kid and things got real." The smile slipped from Rob's face. The room grew both silent and somber. *This guy stays kill'n my vibe!*

"Hold up. I know I asked but It's my birthday, Rob. Let's backtrack," I suggested as I reached for my glass. "Fellas, I made it another year! They said we'd never make it past twenty-five! We can be sad and sh#* tomorrow when we're hung over," I said, lifting my glass to toast. "To a night we will never forget!" Our three glasses clinked and we drank.

We all had our share of regrets. Stuff that didn't go right, or as planned. Life had pressed and stretched us in all different directions. We were all chasing something but this night was not the night for micro pity parties and cocktails. I was going to have fun. My only mission was to hang with my boys and soak up every moment.

"Yo, what time is Phillip getting here?" someone asked.

"He should be pulling up any minute. Have another drink. I want you right by the time we get to the club."

* * *

Rob poured us another generous shot. "So, what are we doing? I feel like bar hop'n. Where are we going?" I asked.

"Does it matter? You ain't driving. All you got to do is have fun," Marlin chimed in.

"Bet! I don't want to be behind the wheel tonight. Ever since my driving while stupid, Uber has been my best friend," I said, smiling like a Cheshire cat.

"And if we get white boy wasted that's exactly what we're going to do," Marlin retorted, grabbing a bag of chips from the pantry.

"Cool."

"Then let's finish this stuff before Phillip gets here. The more we drink here, the less I have to buy you at the club," Rob said as he placed the glasses together to measure out the last bit of Patron between the three of us.

I just shook my head. Rob had always been a cheapskate, even cheaper than me, but now with good reason. He had a kid. I, on the other hand, was supposed to be 'stack'n bread' aka building my savings, but I had been trick'n off. I had bought a house earlier that year, and hadn't yet recovered to a sufficient level for those rainy days my father warned of. To be honest, I often worried about not being in a position financially to support a family. I was finally on my feet, and I was scared of losing everything, but that didn't stop me from buying J's. I know. Not smart.

Phillip arrived as we finished the last of the bottle. I was feeling nice, and from Rob's reddish cheeks, he was too. He climbed into the front seat while I practically fell in the back. I wasn't drunk, but I had a buzz.

"Dang, you guys started to party without me!?!" Phillip cried. His brows furrowed and a scowl took over his face.

Rob patted Phillip on the shoulder as he turned and winked at me. "Man, a party ain't a party until you get there, Phil. Plus, didn't you say you were going to be the designated driver tonight?"

"I said I would drive because you don't know when it's time to go, and E can't drive because it's his birthday."

"Exactly! So, chill, I got you when we get into the club."

I chuckled to myself. Rob was talking like the big man on campus, and we both knew he probably didn't have more than fifty bucks in his pocket. More than likely, Phil and I would end up carrying him before the night was over. For once, I didn't care. It was my birthday; these were my brothers, and I'd put some dough aside specifically for this night.

We were still reminiscing about old times when we pulled up to Krave. Who knew I'd still be friends with my high school chums some ten years later? I wasn't sure what it was at the time. We were as different as night and day, but loyalty kept us together. Especially Rob and I. Rob was selfish. In college, we used to call him "P-town No Favors" because he was the friend you didn't ask to do anything or, in worst-case scenarios, you asked him last. The only reason why we were still friends was because he was the first person to admit it. At least I didn't have to lie to him about it, and he liked the fact that I was able to call him out on his stuff. Phillip was more of a loner. He came around every now and then. The two things I liked about Phillip were that he never showed up to the party empty-handed, and he wasn't the type to call only when he needed something.

Entering the club was like stepping back in time. Familiar faces were shouting my name and embracing me.

"Whoa, what's going on?"

"Surprise!" Rob shouted.

"You threw me a party, bruh?" I felt ashamed. Here I was thinking Rob was a prick, and he went out of his way to get my old friends together for my birthday.

Phillip shook his head. "Nah, this is Mike and Leon's spot. They opened a few months ago and most of the crew hangs here."

Wow. I really was out of the loop. Ever since I got the job in the Public Defender's Office, my lifestyle choices changed. No more late-drunken-nights, no more wild drunken rides through the city, no more drugs. Hanging with the homie just wasn't as important. They were doing the same sh#* just on different days. The same stuff that landed me in jail a couple of times, and I'd had my fill of that.

"First round is on me," Rob shouted over the music.

"This guy," I chirped. Phillip looked at me and smiled as we followed Rob to the bar. I shook my head. Rob was getting his contribution out of the way early because, in typical Rob fashion, he'd disappear and achieve drunkenness by mere proximity. All I could think was, *thank God he isn't our designated driver.*

Rob passed out shots of some purple liquid called *Holy Snickers.* We all took our shot, then I got a cup of beer and approached a group of guys I used to play ball with. I didn't want to admit it, but I was having fun.

"Is that you, Cory? Where the hell you been hiding?" I slapped my old friend hard on the back making him spill some of his drink. Cory was a big one. He was as tall as he was wide, and I could tell he hadn't missed any meals since high school. He turned around slowly, and his face had a grin revealing all the pearly-white teeth he was famous for.

"Estrell! You got some nerve, homie. I heard you had switched sides and was locking brothers up! I think I saw you around the courthouse the other day while I was up there for child support." Cory reached out and grabbed me into a massive hug. I felt like a kid. I was literally inside of this man's chest. I couldn't breathe. The pounds of pressure he applied to my midsection could have easily broken a rib or two, but he soon released me.

"Nah, man. You can't listen to what the streets be saying. My PD work is in service to guys like you. We don't serve them up."

"That's good to know. These days I'm not about that life. I've got too much to lose."

I chuckled. "I feel you, Cory. Me too. How's the fam?"

Our conversation was interrupted by the sight of our friend Chris trotting past carrying the biggest bottle of Patron I'd ever seen. He stopped when he saw me, and I couldn't help but smile.

"Ain't this something? Cory, where did you find this ninja?"

"Don't look at me. He snuck up on me too."

The banter was familiar and pleasant. It's like we didn't even miss a beat. I pointed at the bottle in Chris's hand. "You drinking all of that or are you sharing?"

"Man, ain't nobody stupid enough to try drinking all of this, and if they did, I'd imagine they wouldn't live to tell about it." Chris popped the cork and started pouring.

I didn't want much; I was already lifted, but I wasn't about to turn down a free shot of Patron. Not on my birthday.

"Hold up, man. That's good." I tried to pull back my cup, but Chris continued to pour and that shot became a drink, straight.

"Stop being a pussy!" Both Cory and Chris started laughing, and it felt like they were laughing at my expense. "Are you too good for the juice now?"

"Alright, whatever." And in that moment, I regained some clarity. My memory came back. *This is exactly why I don't mess with y'all anymore.* He filled the red Solo cup to the rim, and I had to take a big swallow just to keep from spilling it everywhere. I had zero intentions of drinking all of it. I eagerly scanned the room for someone else to talk to…an out…an escape. I could feel myself going over the edge.

I walked around the room several times dipping in and out of conversations, nothing serious until I saw Rob again and passed my cup off to him.

"What's this?"

"Patron. Drink wisely, bro."

"Good looking out." Rob raised the cup in salute as I went in search of the bathroom. I was faded.

Chapter Sixteen
Where am I?

My neck was killing me. The muscles spasmed, twitched, and seized sending a shooting pain down the right side of my body; consequences of spending a night with my head awkwardly propped up by a window. My mouth was dry and tasted of hot garbage stewed in *Ciroc*. There was a percussion section of a college marching band stationed just inside my skull— pounding away. I ached all over. It was as if someone had tied my body to the back of a F150 and dragged it across a parking lot covered in speed bumps at a pace slow enough to ensure I struck each one solidly. Squinting, I opened my eyes. The sunlight scorched my retinas with the intensity of a Californian wildfire mixed with teargas. *Okay, where am I?* The dashboard was filthy and unfamiliar. The horse logo in the middle of the steering wheel confirmed what I suspected; I was in an unfamiliar car. *None of my friends drive Mustangs. Whose car is this?*

I sat there in the driver's seat dumbfounded for a second. I hadn't the slightest clue about how I got there and, to put it plainly, I could've been anywhere. The ignition was bare. I found solace in the thought that I hadn't stolen a car and/or driven drunk. *At least I didn't drive.* The last thing I remembered was talking to my friend Danielle by the stage before staggering off to the bathroom. Everything is black after that. *How much did I drink?* I know had a good bit…but damn!

Leaning over, I opened the center console trying to find something that would tell me whose car I was in. For some reason, I wasn't afraid. There had to be a logical explanation for this. I just had to figure it out.

I sifted through various papers and trash, but I found nothing. That's when I looked down and saw that I had my phone. It had some mud on the screen, but other than that, it was still on, and I had about thirty percent left on the battery. I also had seventeen missed calls, twenty-two text messages, and six voicemails all to the effect of "Where the hell are you?" So, I dialed Rob back.

The phone rang one time, and a tap on the window made my heart cease inside my chest. I looked to my left—blue jeans. I scanned upward—dingy white T-shirt and a Caucasian right arm. I thought to myself, *Ohhhh…I bet this is his car.* I could hear him reciting my every move, so instead of looking up at him from my seated position in the car, I decided to get out. He held a cell phone to his left ear as he backpedaled from the door, giving us some space. He looked worried.

* * *

Damn. "Is this your car?" I silently mouthed the words, for I already knew the answer. I had never seen this guy before.

And from the look on his face, he'd never seen me before either. I experienced all the compassion in the world for him in that moment, just imagining what it must've been like to walk outside, first thing in the morning, and finding a big black man posted in your car. He nodded his head yes and spoke into the phone.

"He's out of the car and standing right in front of me now."

"Are you talking to the cops?" I whispered.

He nodded again. This was bad, very bad.

"Hey man, I'm sorry. I didn't mean to scare you, and I wasn't trying to rob you or steal your car. I guess I just needed a place to sleep..." My mind danced through all the possible outcomes and they all concluded with the same answer, *I'm screwed!* I was a black man caught red-handed sitting in a white man's car and I had no clue how I got there. *This isn't going to end well.*

Sirens wailed in the distance. The skin on my forearms tingled from all the adrenaline crawling through my veins. Suddenly, pictures of badged lynch-men, candlelit vigils with built-in curbside makeshift memorials, and R.I.P t-shirts flashed like a slideshow projected before my very eyes. And simultaneously, those same eyes welled with tears and I did the only thing I could think to do, *RUN!*

Now, I should probably tell that this run was not the full-out sprint, complete with chain linked fences, dodging cars and dumpster diving'n, it should have been. It was more of a cautious jog so I could get my bearings and gradually pick up speed once I had a better understanding of my surroundings. *Estrell, where are you?* As my feet thudded against the pavement, I realized I had made yet another mistake. My hungover chubby ass shouldn't have been running. Not in that condition.

My lungs struggled to keep up; I could hear myself wheezing, and there was an extremely painful cramp developing beneath my right rib. *Where are you going? What are you doing? Innocent people don't run, bruh.*

I made it all of about five hundred feet before screeching tires and the front end of a patrol car belonging to Atlanta's finest skidded in front of me and halted my progress. *I'm going to jail.*

"Freeze!"

Instinctively, I threw my hands in the air and closed my eyes. If I was going to die, it wasn't going to be because they thought I was reaching. My legs quivered and fear crept down throat into my exasperated lungs. My shirt trembled as my heart thumped outside of my chest, beating so hard I thought it might explode.

"Don't move, sir."

Her voice struck me like something familiar. I snuck a peek through one eye and instantly, I felt better. *Thank you, Jesus! A black woman. I might not die today after all.*

"It's not what you think, Officer."

The officer guided me to the side of her patrol car. She smelled like sunflowers. "Get on your knees," she commanded. I dropped like I was folding on cotton instead of concrete. The explosion of pain was traumatic. A sharp dagger-like shockwave reverberated through my body. "Do you have anything on you that will stick me, poke me, stab me, cut me, or explode?"

"No, ma'am," I replied as she patted me down.

"Any drugs or narcotics?"

"No, ma'am."

She opened the door to the backseat of her unit, yanked me to my feet, and guided my head as I got in. "Sit tight while we sort this out." She closed the door and walked up the alley from where I had just run.

I heard the squawk of another squad car as it pulled up, stopping abruptly. I wanted to cry, but I was also calm. *Okay. They can charge me with Felony Entering Auto, but they'll lose because they won't be able to prove intent. This isn't Burglary, Theft by Taking or anything of that nature. Worst-case scenario, they'll hit me with mis-demeanor Criminal Trespass. Damn.* I was about to lose everything. Looking out the window, I watched as my entire life, as I knew it, drifted away silently like a submarine be-neath polar ice caps, and I could only think...*Well, you knew it was just a matter of time. But who knew you would go out so epically stupid though?* I was doing so well too.

The patrol officer came back to the car. She got in the driver's seat and slammed the door. Clearly, she was feeling some type of way. "Why are you out here trying to steal people's sh#!*? You scared that man's girl-friend half to death."

Her tone threw me off. *You're way too cute to be cussing at people. Maybe this situation isn't going to be explained away as easily as I thought.* Mistaken, I was sure she was going to understand the uniqueness and complexity of my plight. I mean she was a sista for heaven's sake! I began trying to pump the breaks on the situation.

"Officer, I can explain. I wasn't trying to steal anything. I woke up in that car after going out with the fellas to celebrate my birthday. I guess I blacked out. I'm not saying I think someone put something in my drink, but...I was not trying to steal that car. I got money in my—"

"Shut up! You have the right to remain silent…I suggest you use it."

Her eyes were knife-like, so I exaggerated clamping my lips together. No biggie. I knew the drill. I shouldn't have been running my mouth anyway. It was a moment of weakness because I was trying to avoid being carted off to jail.

For me, life had resembled a *Monopoly* game. I could circle the board and, despite my best efforts, I just couldn't keep that two hundred dollars from passing GO. I'd either hit *Income Tax*, or I'd go straight to *Jail*. This time, going to jail wasn't a metaphor, and I didn't have any more get-out-of-jail-free cards on hand. I'd used them all up. I would be fired and, more importantly, I was going to disappoint everyone who had stuck their necks out for me.

Chapter Seventeen
You're going to jail

*W*here did I go wrong? What the hell happened? Where were my boys? Did I bounce on them? Did they leave me? I wish I'd had a good chance to go through my phone before they caught me. I hung my head and sank my chin down into my chest. These realities were sobering, and weighing it all cleared the fog in my head. My headache went away. In dismay, I stared at my shoes.

WTF? "Seriously? I just bought these!" My shoes dripped with mud. My pants had long dry streaks of Georgia clay and grass stuck to them. My birthday outfit was a mess! *Did I fall? It looks like I stole from second and slid into third base. What the hell happened? I'm too old for this.* It wasn't like me to be so cavalier about my clothes. Especially stuff I had just bought. *At least there's no blood.*

"Didn't I tell you to shut up?"

"Are you taking me to jail?" I didn't have anything else left to lose.

"What do you think?" The officer snickered sarcastically.

I wanted to call her out of her name, but she had a point. She was just doing her job. If I hadn't put myself in this situation, she wouldn't have to.

"Listen, this isn't Entering Auto or Burglary because you can't prove intent. I didn't steal anything. I just woke up there. At best, this is Criminal Trespass. Is there someone I can talk to? Can I speak to a supervisor or something? I'm waiving my rights, and I would like to speak to somebody else." Again, the officer looked at me through the rearview mirror as if my comments confused her, but she didn't respond to me. She radioed a couple of codes, and we were off.

* * *

We pulled up to a satellite office of the Atlanta Police Department off Spring Street and stopped. A surprise since I expected to go straight to the big jail on Rice Street. This, unfortunately, wasn't my first time at a police station, but it felt like it was. The officer took me inside and put me in a room like the interrogation rooms you'd see on *First 48*. The ones with one-way glass, a camera, and everything. Officer Hunter, then, emptied the contents of my pockets into a blue transparent evidence bag and instructed me to sit in a chair on the opposite side of a table. My back was to the wall facing the door. She then cuffed me to the table and left, leaving the door open. This all was a slight improvement from the patrol car. The cuffs had begun to cut into my wrist.

From my seat, I could see the officer at a computer, slowly pecking at the keyboard with her index fingers. *Obviously, they didn't hire her for her typing skills.* She couldn't have keyed more than ten words a minute. *This is going to take all day.* I sat watching her for

140

what seemed like an eternity before two men walked into the room and pulled up some chairs, positioning themselves directly in front of me. The first guy, a middle-aged white man, clearly a detective because of the olive-colored suit from Kohls, the APD lanyard around his neck, and the dry-ass look on his face which read plain as day, 'I need a vacation.' The other guy wasn't as easy to read. He looked as if he had just finished an intense set of dead lifts, and he didn't appear thrilled about the interruption. He, also white, possibly ex-military, was at least ten years senior to the other detective. He wore a gray Born-To-Be-Wild T-shirt, white-washed blue jeans, frayed at the ends from stepping on them with his Sketchers, and his hair…his hair didn't know if it was staying or leaving. It was receding in the front and thinning severely everywhere else. This last bit of information will be important in a moment. Now, I'm not sure if the KKK issues membership cards like the public library, but I'd be willing to bet this guy had a hood in his patrol car.

"What do we have here, Detective? A damn thief. I hate thieves. What's it going to be? Breaking and Entering? Grand Theft Auto?"

"I didn't break into anything, and I didn't try to steal that car," I said emphatically.

"Was I talking to you, boy?"

I bristled but stayed calm. Good cop bad cop was the oldest trick in the book, and this guy was a novice.

Detective Carder answered while thumbing through the police report. "Officer Hunter responded to a call about a black male, fitting this young man's description, rummaging through the complainant's car. As she arrived on the scene, she saw this man trying to flee. She apprehended him a block away."

"Resisting arrest too? Oh, this is getting good. What else you got? Were there any other break-ins in the neighborhood? Unsolved murders? Maybe we can get a twofer."

Murder? Break-Ins? This douche bag had me messed up. "Look, sir, I'll tell you everything I know, but I'm not talking to this prick. He can kick rocks." I pointed at the muscle head with my free hand. It probably wasn't an excellent idea to call him a prick, but I had had enough of his ish. I had nothing to lose. If I was going to drown, he wouldn't be the one holding my head under.

"Sergeant Bass, would you mind grabbing some statement forms?"

The sergeant begrudgingly rose and jeered, "You might want to cuff his other hand; he might try to run again. Or even better...he might try to take a swing at you." He continued with a smirk. "Go ahead, boy. Make my day. Then, I could nail your ass for good."

I could still hear him laughing after he closed the door to the interrogation room.

"I feel sorry for you if you have to deal with that asshole every day."

"You should be feeling sorry for yourself." He was right.

"I didn't break into that man's car. Did you see any broken glass? Did the owner say I took anything?"

"He said you were going through his console."

"I was trying to find out whose car it was! In retrospect, it wasn't the brightest thing to do, but I wasn't trying to steal. I had four hundred dollars in my pocket, some credit cards in my wallet, and the key to MY car for Christ's sake."

"You will not take the Lord's name in vain in my presence."

"I apologize, Detective. I meant no harm. Are you going to send me to jail?"

"Why were you in his car?"

"Honestly, I don't know. I went out with my boys to celebrate my birthday. The last thing I remember was going to the bathroom in the club. After that, everything is blank. When the guy saw me in his car, I had just woken up."

"Right. Where are your friends?"

"Hell if I know."

"What's the name of the club you were at?"

"Krave."

"How did you get to the club?"

"They came and scooped me from the crib. I knew I was going to be drinking, so my boy Phillip was the designated driver."

"I ran your name through our system…"

He didn't even have to finish his sentence. I already knew where he was going. On paper, I look like a bad dude, but I'd changed.

"There are no theft cases on there! I don't steal. And as for the story my rap sheet does tell...I'm not that man anymore. I am a civil servant just as you. I work at the Public Defender's Office. They gave me a chance to turn my life around, and I did. If you take me to jail I will lose everything! They had me on probation for three years. If this gets out, they will fire me. You must believe me. I don't have another comeback in me." I wanted to cry.

"Will your friends back up your story?"

"Yes." I tried to appear confident, but on the inside, I was terrified. I felt like I was being punk'd.

"Write down the names and numbers of your friends and I'll run it by my sergeant."

"That racist? He's one of Trump's foot-soldiers. No doubt about it. He smells like alternative facts."

"You should have thought about that before you got in trouble."

"Trouble seems to find me, sir." I felt dejected.

Detective Carder placed a yellow legal pad in front of me along with a pen, "Write down those numbers."

"I don't know all their numbers by heart, but they are in my phone." I wrote down Rob and Phillip's number as well as the password for my phone.

"Okay. Sit tight," he instructed.

"Really? You've got jokes?"

"Sorry, force of habit."

Chapter Eighteen
What am I talking to you for?

It should have made me feel better that I could see the detective's every move after he walked out, but it didn't. I could hear him leave a message on Rob's voicemail since, ironically, he didn't answer. After this, he picked up and put down the phone at least seven times, but I couldn't read anything on his face. *He would make an excellent poker player.* He got up from his desk without looking in my direction and went into an adjacent office with the sergeant. My mind was racing; flashing images of steel doors and jumpsuits, unemployment lines, EBT, and moving back in with my parents.

In utter disgust, I threw my head down on the table, and I prayed. I prayed for God's grace. I begged for His mercy and salvation. I pleaded for forgiveness and promised everything under the sun, including some things that weren't mine to give away. I prayed until peace radiated through my soul.

"Amen," I whispered.

The door opened. Sergeant Bass walked in smiling, and I had this sinking feeling in the pit of my stomach. "Your friends aren't answering their phones. Too bad they can't back your fairy tale up. Look on the bright side; you won't have to pay for an attorney."

"Are you trying to be funny? You…" I had to put my hand over my mouth to keep from cussing that bastard out. There wasn't anything I could do to convince him I was innocent. *Screw it. God help me.*

Sergeant Bass left the door open when he came back in to gloat, so it had to have been a divine fiat from the heavens when I heard the phone ring and someone yelled, "Did anyone call a Robert Phillips?" I could feel the clouds begin to part exposing the sun. I watched through the door as Detective

Carder crossed the room and took the call. I listened intently as he rattled off questions to corroborate my story before thanking Rob and hanging up the phone. He turned and came into the room just as Sergeant Bass took a seat at the table.

"So, you had a night on the town with friends to celebrate your birthday. At some point during the festivities, you black out and wake up in that poor guy's car. Witnesses say they see you going through the center console. Police nab you at the scene. We caught you red-handed. On top of that, there's no one who can confirm your side of the story. Does that about sum it up? What am I missing?" Detective Carder, who was standing in the doorway scrolling through his phone, sat down while Sergeant Bass was patronizing me. He didn't say a word, but I knew. I knew he had just confirmed my 'fairy tale' and that Sergeant *Rogaine* here had just placed his foot firmly in his mouth.

"What am I missing?" He repeated as if we didn't hear him the first time.

"Other than your hairline? You have it all."

Detective Carder lost all composure. His pale face became flush, and his eyes watered from laughing so hard. He pointed at Bass as he cackled, giving no sanctuary to his embarrassment and leaving no room for retort.

"He got you good, Sarg!"

The sergeant's face had grown flush too. He tapped his fingers on the table. He appeared to be calculating his next move.

"Ha ha ha," he muttered.

"Well…" the detective said wiping his face as he tried to gather himself, "…I just spoke to one of your friends, and your story checks out." He reached into his pocket, retrieved keys to the cuffs, and unshackled me.

"So ya'll aren't moving forward with the charges?" I said rubbing my wrist.

"Technically, you were never arrested. But charging you isn't our decision to make."

"Then why am I talking to you!?! Whose decision is it?"

"That'll be up to the arresting officer, Officer Hunter."

"Her?" I exclaimed, pointing out of the open door toward the computer station where she sat, still typing away.

"Yep."

I slid my chair away from the table, positioning it just in front of the wall facing the door. I then pressed my foot against the wall and used it to propel myself through the door, across the room, and right up next to Officer Hunter.

* * *

"The Detective confirmed what I told you," I began, trying not to sound overly confident about my impending freedom. "You should kick me loose and go get your hands dirty with some real criminals."

"Is that right? What part of being found rummaging through someone's car doesn't make you a criminal? Humph?"

"Officer Hunter, have you ever made a mistake in your life? Something you must carry around with you every single day like a permanent backpack, or just a tacky shirt you can't take off? I have. I have made more mistakes than I can count, but I've never made the same mistake twice. I am not asking you for a miracle. I am asking you for a small amount of mercy."

"I'm sorry, Mr. Young."

"I understand." I sat back and began to spin myself around and around in my chair.

"If you want to plead your case to my supervisor, I'll let you. Letting you go will have to be his call."

I perked up. "I do! Where is he?"

Officer Hunter picked up the phone, dialed a couple of numbers, and muttered something like, "Will you come down here for a second?" Those few moments between the jarring thud of the receiver kissing the base, and the arrival of the custodian of my fate, felt like an eternity. I really can't explain my heightened sensory awareness. Everything was so amplified, from the sound of the clamoring voices emanating from the squad room to the smack of Officer Hunter's watermelon Bubblicious. I even imagined her supervisor pushing back from his desk, the wheels scraping against the floor, the leather chair exhaling as he rose, a pen rolling across the top of his otherwise pristine desk. His recently-polished shoes clip-clapping and slapping the floor as he hastened his stride to answer the call of his underling. My heart was orchestrating the woodwind section of a symphony with the blood flowing through my veins. The ding of the elevator announced his arrival. *This is it.* The doors rattled as they rolled open and "The Man" emerged. The brother was sharp; decorated like a war veteran dressed for a funeral; Lord, please don't let it be mine. *This is it.* Sweat dripped like pellets against my shirt. I closed my eyes and counted to ten trying to slow my beating heart. He traversed the room with an air of power, garnering formal and informal greetings, salutes, and stares from all who saw. Officer Hunter, who stood once his highness entered the room, relinquished her chair so he could sit next to me.

"What's going on?"

"Good morning, sir. I'm going to make this short and sweet. I know you guys are busy. My name is Estrell Young, and I am an investigator in the Newton County Public Defender's Office. Last night, I went out with a group of friends to celebrate my 25th birthday. Long story short, this morning I woke up in a white man's car, and now I'm here. I did not break in or steal anything but, nonetheless that's a crime. The detectives have confirmed everything I just told you. It was an honest mistake. Everyone here thinks I should be let go, and we just need you to sign off, boss."

He skimmed through what I assumed to be Officer Hunter's report as I spoke. At the end, he placed it on the desk, got up, and walked over to her. He whispered something in her ear, and just as he did minutes before, he floated away.

"Where's he going?" I asked frantically.

"Stand up, Mr. Young."

"Hey! Excuse me, sir! Please!"

"Estrell, calm down." Officer Hunter handed me the blue bag holding my personal effects.

"So, I'm free to go?" I looked up and mouthed thank you toward the ceiling. Later, I would get on my knees and sing His praises the right way.

"Yes. Stay out of trouble."

"I sure will, ma'am. Thank you for everything."

"Don't thank me. I was just doing my job."

I hit the front door at a pace you'd consider to be a little more than a trot. I wanted to get as far away from the police station as I could as quickly as possible. I turned on my phone. There was only seven percent battery life remaining, so I had to make my calls count. I called Rob.

"Yo, I need you to come pick me up. I'm at the Atlanta Police Station downtown off Spring?"

"Well, I haven't got my clothes on, and I got to—" I hung up on him. *Ridiculous.* He didn't even ask me why I arrested. When people show you who they are, you should believe them. I made a mental note to remove him from the short list of people I considered friends. I called my sister. As much as I wanted to keep this whole ordeal a secret, I needed help, and I knew she would give it unconditionally. After all, I prayed and everything.

"Wow. That was a close one!"

Looking Back

Chapter Nineteen
I hate Facebook

As I hunched over my keyboard trying to evoke words to convey my dismay with the subject matter of my latest entry, I realized I was in my feelings heavy. This always happened when I was passionate about something. Shrugging my shoulders, I tried to shake the anxiety as I wrote:

I hate Facebook. And not in a way that can be minimized or surmised as something else— I hate it. All my friends are happy— on a beach somewhere, nestled in the bosom of their soul mate, skydiving, doing something ratchet, eating something amazing, proposing or getting married, buying houses or cars, in a club somewhere popping all the bottles and listening to the hottest new music, and earning all the money. I hate Facebook. This is depressing. I should be doing more. My life sucks. Or, at least, these are the thoughts and feelings I am left with once I've finished scrolling down my timeline, and I discard the empty bottle of Moscato sitting on the kitchen counter and move on to something stronger. Period.

The crisp tick of that last keystroke snapped me out of the trance of lamenting. *I should take a break.* I placed my laptop on the coffee table and walked into the kitchen.

"Hey babe, where's that bottle of Crown Apple I bought last week?"

Without looking up from the magazine she was reading, she said, "We finished it the day before yesterday."

"That's right," I mumbled closing the cabinet door.

"There's some sangria in the fridge," She-rice suggested as she entered the room. I felt her come to rest behind me. She got close.

158

She wrapped her short arms around my waist, nuzzled her face between my shoulder blades, and inhaled deeply.

"You want some?" I asked.

"Yes, please." She didn't move. And we stood there, occupying the same space, her clinch tightening, enfolding my midsection. "Are you okay?"

"Yeah."

"Are you sure?"

"I'm good," I insisted, turning to place the wine on the counter.

"Every time you get on Facebook your mood changes. It's like you sink into yourself. Memory lane becoming a bit too much?"

"No, I just have a lot going on, and spending time on Facebook is something I'd rather not be doing. Marketing sucks, but I need to build momentum until my book release party."

"I know why you're back on. I'm curious about whether it's what is affecting you or something. Why did you get off in the first place?"

"Several reasons. I didn't have a filter, and I was immature."

"I can see that."

"It's impersonal, and I felt myself losing the ability to communicate face-to-face."

"I don't believe it. You're a talker, and you'll always be a talker."

"Whatever. And you're a jerk," I countered with a chuckle.

"Any other reasons?"

"It was depressing. You know, there needs to be a degree of separation between the haves and the have-nots. When you're broke, and struggling, you don't want to see your friends, and even people you hate, ball out."

"How long were you off again?" she asked, turning and going back into the living room as if we weren't in the middle of a conversation.

Glasses in hand, I slothfully followed her. Sherice, my girlfriend, a recent college grad and aspiring professional gymnast, sprawled across my chocolate leather sectional watching TV. She lifted her thick legs so I could reinstate myself beneath them and continue where I left off. "Eleven years."

"That's a long time. How are you handling it all? Do you find yourself immersed in the lives of people you haven't seen in ages?"

"I'm trying not to do that," I say with a chuckle. "It's difficult, but I keep telling myself I'm only back on here for one reason, to promote these books."

"That's right. I don't have to worry about you getting distracted by old flames, do I? You and these girls are going to try to 're-connect'…"

"Yoooooo, that is definitely something I'm going to have to get used to or do something about. I am far more accessible than I care to be. I need at least two layers of protection from random people IM'ing me. Like with text messages, I enjoy knowing a person doesn't know if I read their text or not. I need to fix that on here asap."

"You can manage that in your settings."

"Thanks."

Sherice grabbed the remote and increased the volume by a smidge on her favorite show, *I Love Lucy*. She had an affinity for Lucille Ball that is parallel to none.

Chapter Twenty
Friend Request

The volume of the TV crept up until Lucille Ball's annoying voice began to drown out my thoughts. I looked at Sherice to express my displeasure.

"Hey…"

"Shhhhhhhhh. This is the good part!"

I turned my attention back to my computer. Picking it up, I noticed I had two new friend requests. I toggled the button with the cursor, and the drop-down opened displaying the request. Uncle Jeff from the Rickey Smiley morning show, who I idolize immensely, and Tonya Spellman. At once, I became flooded with emotion. *No way!*

"Holy sh*#!" I exclaimed, tossing Sherice's mocha-colored legs to the side as I stood up on the couch, jumping up and down excitedly.

"What? Baby, what is it?!" Sherice stood, her voice rising to an octave matching mine. "Tell me!"

"Uncle Jeff just requested my friendship on Facebook!"

"Uncle Jeff? Who is Uncle Jeff?" she asked as she sank back down on the sofa, clearly disinterested.

"Baby! He's only the greatest motivational speaker and political pundit in the world!" I jumped again for emphasis. This was truly a praise-worthy event for me, and I was basking in it.

"You should stop jumping on that before you break it."

"Sherice, you just don't understand; this is epic! If I could get on his show or put a copy of my book in his hand, it would be crazy!"

"You're weird. Get down."

I climbed down, and with the same level of emotional intensity, just completely opposite of elation, I noted who the other request was from.

"That's not all; Tonya Spellman wants to be my friend too..."

"You do realize Facebook friendship isn't 'real' friendship, right?"

"Your point?"

"Don't be so dramatic. Who is Tonya Spellman anyway? If y'all used to date, don't tell me."

I had her full attention now. It almost sounded like she was jealous. A part of me liked it, so I placed my laptop down and turned toward Sherice. Her brown eyes fixed on mine, searching, examining every inch of my pupils. Her head tilted slightly as to angle her tiny ears to catch every word. I smiled.

"Who is she, Estrell?" she hissed, losing all semblance of patience.

"Do you remember my telling you about getting suspended in elementary school?"

"For the fire? Yeah."

"See...I didn't get expelled for the fire. I was expelled for bringing a box cutter to school and, allegedly, threatening to kill this chick, Tonya Spellman. She testified at my hearing, and that lie could've ruined my life!" Just like that, all the hatred I had for her came rushing back.

"Ahhhhh, now I remember. But I'm pretty sure the fire is the part of that story that did you in."

"Whatever. You don't know nuffin," I muttered. She would never be able to understand, so I didn't even bother to try to explain it to her.

The room grew silent. We both sipped sangria while I reconciled my emotions and tried to finish my blog post. *I really hate Facebook*. Just as I was about to conclude my rant, I received another notification.

Chapter Twenty-One
Facebook Messenger

Bing. Sherice looked at me, but I didn't reciprocate. This wasn't just a friend request, it was an instant message, which are the devil by the way. How is it someone thought it apropos to create a messaging service where the sender is notified or can see when the recipient has seen it? That's just wrong on so many levels. I started to close it without reading it until I realized who it was from.

Sherice placed her hand on my knee and shook it gently.

"Estrell…what's wrong? Your whole demeanor changed. Did Tonya send you a message?"

"Man, what is it about today?! This can't be real. Somebody must be prank'n me. There is no way, of all nights, I get a message from her."

"Who?" Sherice leaned over to peek at the screen, but I put my body between us. My heart was racing.

"This has to be a joke. Someone is trying to be funny, but I'm not amused." I clicked the icon, and it expanded in the bottom corner of the screen.

"You're scaring me."

"Chill."

"Hell nah, I'm not going to chill! Who is it from?"

"Babe, it's from my old teacher, Ms. Linangrass. What in the world is going on?"

"Your elementary school teacher?"

I didn't trust myself to speak, so I nodded my head. I felt my eyes begin to tingle. My tear ducts swelled.

"What did she say?"

I handed her the computer.

Dear Estrell,

You may not remember me, but I definitely remember you. I taught you, briefly, when you were in the fourth grade. You changed my life, and it settles my heart to see you are doing well. I'm overjoyed about the man you've become!

I have been an educator for twenty-two years now, and I must admit, it was your time at Marbut that resonated with me the most. You, Estrell, with your bright eyes and wide smile, used to light up a room. And, foolishly, I allowed my feelings about your misbehavior to overshadow one enormously important fact; I didn't know how to teach you.

I was so consumed with the appearance of running an orderly and respectful class I forgot to teach.

So, I feel like I failed you, Estrell. I felt like we just threw you away. And I have carried the weight of that thought with me, like a purse, ever since. As I said previously, you changed my life. That situation influenced the way I have handled every single child I've had the privilege to teach, even my own. I believe in a higher power, and I've prayed and everything that one day I'd have an opportunity to say this to you and return the favor.

I am now principal at Marbut Theme School. We are having a commencement ceremony at school, and I know you don't owe me any favors, and probably haven't given this school much thought over the years...but if you did...it would be an honor to have you come back and share your story with our student body. It would mean so much to me personally. You are a true inspiration. Let me know what you think.

Warmest regards, Dr. Linangrass

"Wow, that is so nice," Sherice said as she looked up at me from the screen. Her eyes grew wide as she took in the tears that had been flowing down my face. I tugged at my shirt and used it to wipe my face. I felt like my eyes were puffy and red, and my voice cracked when I spoke.

"I always thought she hated me."

"Well, you have that effect on people," she joked, putting my laptop down beside her.

"See..."

"What? Too soon? My bad?"

Shaking my head, I mumbled, "I'm sorry."

"For what?"

"Crying."

"Boy bye. Today has been a rough day. From what you've told me, it seems like it was inevitable that you'd end up right here."

"Yeah, things have been tugging at me from all directions and that..." I said pointing to my computer, "...is the icing on the cake."

"So, who was she to you?"

"Ms. Linangrass? She was one of the best teachers I've ever had. But it just always seemed like I caught her at an inconvenient time. Or, like I got on her nerves. She would make me stand in the corner of the room for hours."

"Are you going to go back?"

I scooted to the edge of the couch and grabbed my cell phone off the coffee table. "I have to call my mom."

"It's ten o'clock."

"She's up. Watch," I replied tapping the screen to make the call.

The phone rang one time.

"Hello?"

"Hey, Mom."

"Hi, baby."

"Sorry to bother you so late…"

"No biggie. I just finished watching Big Brother. What's up?"

"Do you remember Ms. Linangrass?"

"That name sounds familiar. Is that one of your teachers from high school?"

"Elementary school."

"Panola Way?"

"Nope. Marbut."

"The lady who got you expelled?!" she bleated.

"That's the one."

"Yeah, I remember that old bag. What about her? She could've ruined your life, you know."

"Mom, I'm pretty sure I was more to blame for that than she was."

"You're probably right. I just hate they gave up on you so easily."

"Apparently, she's been feeling the same way for the past twenty-plus years. She sent me a message on Facebook. And guess who had the nerve to send me a friend request…"

"Who?"

"Tonya Spellman."

"Who is that?"

"The girl from Marbut!"

"The one who said you threatened to kill her?" she gasped.

"That's the one."

"All of this happened tonight?"

"In a matter of minutes, Mom."

"The universe is trying to tell you something, boy. What did the teacher want?"

"To apologize. She's the principal over there now."

"Is that right?"

"Yep. And she wants me to come back and speak to the kids."

"Get out of here! Won't HE do it?! Are you going to go? I definitely want to be in the building for that."

"I'm thinking about it."

"There is nothing to think about, Estrell. You better go back there and share your story with those kids. Is she going to pay you?"

"We haven't discussed any of the details. I haven't even responded to her message yet." I stood up and walked to the window. The street, barely illuminated; the sky peppered with stars.

"You should do it. And your book is about to be released too! The timing seems ordained. That should be your first stop on your book tour. That would be an amazing way to finish your story."

"I'm going to do it."

"Yay!" The ladies cheered in unison as if Sherice, who was eavesdropping from the couch, and my own mother were sharing a wavelength. "Who is that in the background?"

"You know who that is."

"Tell Sherice I said hey!" I could hear her smiling through the phone. "Can I come?" asked my mom.

"Why not? I started this journey with you; might as well end it right."

"Yes! This is so exciting. I can't wait to post this on Facebook!"

"Don't do that, Mom. Go sit down somewhere! Listen, I must go. I will talk to you later. I love you, bye."

"Congrats again, baby."

I hung up the phone, and Sherice was staring at me. The energy in the room had lifted, and it felt good. It felt like the FDA had issued an apology and admitted something was wrong with "government cheese," or the CIA took responsibility for the crack epidemic. Better yet, it was like you always knew something was a bit off with you, and your mom finally admitted to dropping you shortly after your birth because she was drugged up in the hospital bed and the nurse forgot to pull up the rails. Everything was starting to make sense now.

"I think a celebration is in order," she pronounced as she walked toward me.

"Maybe later, babe. I want to message Ms. Linangrass back first."

Chapter Twenty-Two
Where it all began

O ver the next couple of weeks, Ms. Linangrass and I corresponded regularly, ironing out the details and arranging things for my visit.

The morning of the program, my mom met me in front of the school, and we walked in, hand in hand, just like the way we left almost twenty-three years prior; the only difference was this time I held my head high.

"Good morning, Mr. Young."

"Good morning, Dr. Linangrass. That has a nice ring to it," I replied as I reached to meet her outstretched hand. She looked virtually the same; give a pound or two here and there, a few more wrinkles, and some gray. "You remember my Mother, don't you?"

"Of course, I do! How are you doing, Mrs. Young?"

"It's McKinney now, but whatever," she corrected with a nervous smile. My mother, clearly more excited than I, was glowing.

"My apologies. Right this way. This morning we have two hundred and four students graduating, and another two hundred or so who are here to see you. We also have parents, other various family members, faculty, and staff. You have a full house."

"Wow. That's wonderful. Can I have a glass of water?" My stomach was in knots. My heart, seeming to have started the fight-or-flight sequence prematurely in my opinion, was in full-blown pound mode now.

"Sure. We have a room all set up with a breakfast bar and refreshments for you and your mother. The program will start in about twenty minutes. Coach Adams is going to speak first…"

"Coach Adams is still here?" I coughed.

"Yep. He and I are still going strong."

"That's impressive."

"After he finishes, he will introduce me, and I will introduce you. You will have an hour to do your thing."

"Sounds good."

The halls, a miniature replica of my memory, with walls painted white smoke and Spanish gray floors, smelled like bleach and opportunity. Every step, a corresponding flashback, a chorus of nostalgia, an ode to time gone by, was breathtaking. I nearly threw up when we got to the room they'd had set up for us; Coach Adams's old office.

"Here we are."

"So, you got jokes, Dr. Linangrass."

"I thought you'd be comfortable here," she remarked confidently, as if my response had met the mark.

"Mom, this is Coach Adams's office, and that's the door to the bathroom where I set the fire," I announced pointing to the door in the corner."

"Really!" she chuckled. "Ms. Linangrass, you are all right."

"Thank you, Mrs. Young. You guys make yourselves comfortable, and someone will come for you in about thirty minutes."

"Dr. Linangrass…" I started as she began to close the door. "How's your heart now?"

My question caught her off guard. She, standing there in the doorway, corrected her posture and placed a finger over her lips. Her sniffle sliced through the silence.

"Ask me when this is over." And with that, she closed the door and was gone. I walked over to the beverages while my mother put down the thirty-six camera bags she brought along for the occasion. I placed my note cards on the table and cracked open a ginger ale, taking a sip, and the carbonation settled the rumble right away.

"Yo, they have fruit, bougie cheese, crackers, and juice!'

"Estrell, are you ready for this?"

"Ummmm…yeah. A piece of cake," I lied.

"I mean, I would be crapping bricks if it were me."

"Well, it's not you, Mom. So, please. Give me a moment to gather my thoughts."

"Well, excuse me," she mouthed, turning her attention back to the cameras.

"I didn't mean to snap at you. But I don't want to play one hundred questions before I go out there and talk to these kids about the future."

"Understandable. And I'm not going to pepper you with questions, but let me say this. I am so proud of you. You've come so far, grown so much, done so well. Today, you have made it. It is, in and of itself, the end of a chapter and the beginning of a brand new one. Your grandfather would've been proud too. I pray he's looking down on you right now."

Before I could respond, there was a knock at the door, and we were ushered off. I don't recall much from the walk to the gym because we got to the gym so fast, but when I parted ways with my mother and climbed the stairs onto the stage, I felt a calm take over me.

Chapter Twenty-Three
Let's Talk

D r. Linangrass was at the podium, and I am not going to lie to you and say I heard any part of my introduction. The sea of faces, some young and some old, was far too captivating. I don't even remember hearing the applause. The only thing that is still with me from the beginning of my speech is the sheer panic I felt when I realized I had left my note cards on the table in Coach Adams's office.

Well, here goes nothing:

"Wow, thank you Dr. Linangrass for your kind words. Bear with me; I need a moment. I never in a million years thought I would be back in this school, and on this stage. It's...overwhelming."

I could feel sweat dripping from my underarms, and I was thankful for the suit I was wearing. It would prove useful in ways other than affording my speech legitimacy; it would help disguise the rings forming under my armpits. I knew I was going to be nervous. I hadn't prepared for any of the other sentiments that flooded my senses once upon that stage.

Okay, I'm ready...I can't tell you what an honor it is for me to take this stage as you prepare for the next phase of your lives. I didn't get the opportunity to cross it as you will, and I hope your walk will be a lot different from mine. But even though we won't share a path, I am living proof that things do come full circle. You see, I started out here. I was here when the doors opened. And at the time, I did not know how to NOT take this opportunity for granted. I

181

didn't see it as a chance at better. I saw this place as a barrier between my friends and me. I used to go to school up the road and my mother, who is here today, stood in line for eight hours so I could have a chance at a better life. I thought she was a vicious dictator. So, I squandered it. I wasted the chance, and I wasn't here long. My choices took me far away from here, and put my life on a course similar to those kids you see on Scared Straight. But I'm not here to talk to you about that today. Today, I'm here to talk to you about three things you should keep in mind as you prepare to leave this place for different pastures. Three things you will inevitably run into as you traverse this thing called life. I promise to keep this brief, but they are as follows: First, I'm going to talk to you about ignoring your feelings. Second, we'll cover why you should never shy away from failure. And lastly, we will talk about how to focus on others because service will keep you happy. Feelings, Failure, and Focus.

Chapter Twenty-Four
Feelings

I'd like to start by reading the scrip-
ture upon which I have based how I
live my life. It can be found in Acts
20:24, and it reads:

"But my life is worth nothing to me unless
I use it for finishing the work assigned to
me by the Lord Jesus—the work of telling
others the Good News about the wonderful
grace of God."

Growing up, I was told I was a bad kid. Very smart, advanced for my age, good with words but, undeniably, I was bad. I felt bad. No one expected much out of me so I did and said terrible things. Bad was a label I took on, and my behavior reflected it. But when it comes to labels, you should be careful about which ones you choose to embrace. Allowing labels to define you, especially the negative ones, can cause you to act and to feel in ways that fit that label. Once you repeat an act so many times, it becomes a habit. Ladies and gentlemen, habits define who you are, and shape your feelings about yourself. I want each of you to be careful because you can become a product of feel.

Feelings are tricky. When it comes to feelings, nothing is a mathematical certainty. You may be asking what I mean when I say that. Well, here's what I mean; 1+1=2, that is a mathematical certainty. There is no "unless." Now, think about one of your friends, one of your best friends, and think about all the great feelings and memories you have when you think about them. Are you with me? Now, think about a time when they made you mad, but they really didn't do anything to you. Think about how you felt. Think about the intensity of that emotion, not because of something they did, but because of how you felt at the time. Maybe you were hungry or tired. That's what I mean. Depending on what lens you use to look at something, feelings can be unreliable. In that instance, just because they made you feel some type of way, it doesn't rewrite the friendship or make them a horrible person, even though that may be how you feel. Those feelings are temporary, and you should ignore them. You can manage your feelings. Manage those feelings. When I was a kid, and they told me I was "bad," I had an opportunity to NOT take that label personally, and think about it in the context of what they were talking about, my behavior at the time. It didn't mean I was a bad person, who no one wanted around and who was unworthy of love. But feelings can make you feel that way. And that's the first part of the Good News I'm here to share with you today. You can ignore your feelings.

You can manage your emotions. You can choose not to allow the world to define you. You can define yourself! Just because you failed a test doesn't make you a failure. Just because you stole something, you're not a thief. Just because something bad happened to you, you aren't a victim. It took me thirty-one years to understand that last part, and I'll touch on it again later in my closing. But I need you to understand you have a choice.

Chapter Twenty-Five
Failure

Secondly, I want to share with you my thoughts on failure. Michael Jordan, the greatest basketball player of all time, was cut from his high school basketball team. Oprah Winfrey was fired from her first TV job. Everyone fails. Do you know how many times Steve Jobs, Bill Gates, and Mark Zuckerberg got it wrong before getting it right? Failure is the start to every great accomplishment. Einstein said, *"Failure is success in progress."* It is the place where you learn what doesn't work! There is nothing better than having some experience to pull from. Ladies and gentlemen, I wrote two books before anyone ever thought about inviting me anywhere. I have spoken at events, and it went so badly that I wasn't invited back. I've been booed! But, to quote the fallen star, Aaliyah, if at first you don't succeed…dust yourself off and try again. Failure makes people stronger. Learn your lessons, apply them, and try again. Can you imagine living a life having never ridden a bike because you quit? Quitting should never be an option. So, never shy away from failure.

When I graduated from college, I was virtually unemployable in my career field. I got in some trouble during my time there. It was a rough period for me, newly entering the world a grown man and I had nothing to stand on. Nothing to build with because I perceived my tools to be useless since I couldn't use my degree. I even got fired from the one job I did have. At the time, I was a cook at Applebee's and I was good at it! I tried to learn all the cook stations because you received a dollar raise per station you knew. I was doing well, until one night the manager asked me to wash dishes. "To-night, I need you to be my GU," he said. GU stands for general utility, and it means dishwasher. So, I washed dishes that night, and I guess I did a decent job. Because the next night when I came in to work, the schedule had changed, and my name was under GU for every day for the rest of the month. I had become a full-time dishwasher overnight. And I'll admit; it bothered me. Not because I was better than doing dishes, but because it was the least respected position in the establishment. I was prideful. After one too many dowsing's with murky dishwater and salad dressing, I gave some young waitresses a taste of the water hose. Not my proudest moment. Consequently, I no longer had a job and had to move back home, in with my father. Can you imagine how that felt? There I was, a grown man living with my father like we were roommates or something. But I couldn't even say that because I wasn't paying any bills. It was all bad. Here is where I want to talk about shifting focus. The universe has a funny way of suggesting that you change your perspective.

Chapter Twenty-Six
Focus

gain, there I was, grown, unem-
ployed, living with a parent,
thousands of dollars in student
loan debt, bill collectors calling daily, and a
criminal case pending. I had all these hopes
and dreams, things I wanted to accomplish,
but I was going nowhere. I knew I was
destined for greatness but I was doing noth-
ing. It felt as if I were in an airplane over
Hartsfield and I couldn't land, and I
couldn't fly off to another destination. I
couldn't start my life. So, I became de-
pressed. I started to drink more often. I
spent a lot of nights at the bottom of a bot-

tle and, eventually, my father had had enough. One Friday morning, after an epic night of drinking, he slid a business card underneath my door. It was the card of the Chief Public Defender for the Alcovy Judicial Circuit, and on it was a message, "Whoever wants to be a leader among men must first be a servant." That one act by my father changed the trajectory of my story. I made the call. I interviewed and I got to work.

Two months into my internship, I met a young woman. And this woman was in jail for the thirty-seventh time. She, a cocaine addict who also abused alcohol, admittedly, needed help. But, this time she was innocent. She told me a story. She was living with her sister, and one night she came home from work and found her lying in the corner of their trailer, and her husband was on top of her, beating her savagely. So, my client did what any good sister would do; she came to her defense, and she stabbed him. This stopped the assault and probably saved her sister's life. But her sister didn't see it that way, and when the cops got there, she sided with her husband. Thus, my client was arrested. Now, I won't go into detail about the trial process because it's a long story, but based on things I found during my investigation, we won the case. In any other scenario, that young lady would have been able to go home; not in this one though. She ended up going to prison for three years because she had messed up prior to her arrest for the stabbing. The arrest itself meant a violation for her, and I was devastated. I went to go and see her, and my emotions got the best of me. I was crying and screaming about fairness and the system, and you know what? She was calm. She said, "Mister Young, you saved my life. No one has ever believed in me and fought for me the way you did. Thank you." This blew my mind. It shifted my focus. I had found my purpose. From that day forward, I got proximate. I got close to people who were hurting more than me, and being of service to them saved my life, guys. There's a whole world out there of people who need you. As the coming days unfold, you're going to be deciding what your life's work *will be and once you decide, I want you to set out to do it and do it well. We are all counting on you.*

So, in closing, there's going to come a time in each of your lives when things are going to go bad. In those moments, I urge you to do the three things we've talked about here today. First, get proximate and shift your focus. Second, ignore your feelings. You are NOT the sum of the worst things you've ever done, nor of the things that have happened to you. You're not. And last of all, get up every day, place one foot in front of the other, and fail again. Perfection is impossible, so just move forward—progress. That's what I'm going to do.

The crowd erupted. Dr. Linangrass, who had gone down and sat next to my mother, met me at the bottom of the stage with a hug. She pulled me into her chest so my ear was right in front of her mouth and said, "Ask me again."

I looked at her and complied with her request.

"How is your heart now, Dr. Linangrass?"

"Filled full, Estrell. Filled full."

Dr. Linangrass grabbed my hand and together we stood in front of that student body, basked in the shower of applause, and relished the moment. She lifted my hand in victory, sparking an even greater ovation. My mother came and joined us, eyes puffy and red. It was one the best moments of my life.

People ask me how I ended up here and the answer is simple...I don't know. But, *I prayed and everything.*

The End

Epilogue

2:14 a.m.

The phone rang. I didn't hear it. Besides being in a coma, when I'd stumbled to bed, I'd tossed it in the direction of my nightstand. I took note of the thump it made when it landed on the carpet.

My smart watch woke me. I crawled over to the side of the bed and retrieved the phone from the floor. The screen, now cracked. *Damn it.*

"Hello?"

Silence. I pulled the phone away from my ear to examine it. Through squinted eyes, I read the caller ID: Mom Dukes.

"Mom, are you there?" I could hear her breathing, and I could hear something else. It took a minute, but I got it.

"Is he gone?" I pushed myself upright because I already knew the answer.

Switching the phone from one ear to the other, I ran my hand down the side of my face and across my chin.

"Mom?"

"Yeah…Estrell he's—" She whimpered. "He's gone, baby."

Her voice was faint. She drew a breath and, instead of gradually succumbing to the grief, gut wrenching wails filled the distance between us. I placed my head in my hand. I had no words. Tears spilled from my eyes and dribbled through the cracks of my fingers and down my forearms. The plastic of my phone case crunched. I loosened my grip.

I had been bracing for this moment for months, but I wasn't ready.

"Are you okay?"

It was a stupid question. The instant the words broke free from my lips I tried to catch them. The wheels had come off the wagon. *Hell nah, she isn't okay. How could she be?* My mother had assumed the role of caregiver, attendant, chauffer, and nurse. She was ground zero.

I spun my legs over the side of the bed and slid my bare feet across the carpet. *You knew, didn't you? You felt this coming.* I managed to box in my sorrow by not thinking about it.

"So, what's next? Where is grandma?"

My mother blew her nose to muster the smallest amount of composure.

"She's in the bed with him."

"What?"

"The hospice nurse told her to take some time to say goodbyes while we wait on the coroner."

"They're not sending an ambulance?"

"We don't need one, Estrell."

"I'm on my way."

I was already halfway down the stairs when she said, "No, baby. There's nothing you can do here. And, I don't want you driving."

"Mom, I'm coming." I hung up the phone, turned around, and went back to my room, because I didn't even have a shirt on.

I staggered into the closet to grab a shirt and some socks. These basic tasks were a chore.

I prayed. *"God, I need your help. I need to sober up."* Then, as if a film director had signaled it, my mother's words replayed in my head. "There's nothing you can do here." And that was it. As those words reverberated over and over, everything I'd held back came crashing down.

Photographs, snap shots, flashes of memories falling like credits before my eyes. A spool of film, recounting into a collage what my grandfather meant to me. His life, intrinsically intertwined with mine since my beginning, had meant everything. The enormity of such a loss was indescribable.

All the emotions and fears that had been gnawing at me since I picked up the phone took root. My eyes purged every ounce of water from my body. Snot and slobber, or a mixture of the two, hung from my chin. There was too much going on. I placed my hands on the wall and took deep breaths. My insides twisted the more I thought about it. I moved to the other side of the closet desperately trying to suck in more air.

Instinctively, I tilted my head back. My legs were noodles. They gave way and I fell backward, taking entire top shelf of the closet with me. I laid there on the floor, beneath collared shirts and shelving, until I cried myself to sleep. I vaguely remember talking to my mom again. I told her I wasn't going to be able to make it and I'd see her tomorrow. I also remember seeing my Grandpa smile. He might have whispered, "Good idea, Chief."

My compass was gone. My grandfather, the model I rolled after, the shoes my feet weren't big enough to fill, the fulcrum on which my family propped itself was no more. And I was lost.

For months, it rained death. With his exit, a floodgate opened and the waters of mortality flowed out. I lost friends and other family members in rapid succession. I'd hardly recover from one funeral before I had to attend another.

The wheels had come off the wagon. Between funerals and wakes, drunken brawls and hangovers, I was struggling to keep it all together. I was teetering on the edge of destruction. By December, something was going to have to give or I'd lose everything.

December 29, 2015
9:37p.m.

The phone rang. As it always does when you don't want to be bothered.

"Hello?"

"What's up my guy? How you doing over there?"

"I can't call it, Dre. What's good?" I responded, uncorking the bottle of single malt Scotch I had been tapping for the past two hours.

"I hear that, man. I've been out of it since Pete's funeral. His family has been keeping me busy, though. I just got home from taking his daughters to get winter coats."

"That's what's up. How's his wife?" I say taking a swig straight from the bottle.

"Struggling, bro. He was everything to her and for him to go out like that, without warning, to just be gone is...I don't know, man. We're all going through it right now. But I didn't call to talk about them. What's up with you? What's this I hear about you out here wild'n, choking people out and fighting in the club? That's not you, homie."

Plyers in hand, his question stripped my wire coating and exposed raw nerve. "I don't know, man. I guess I wanted to hit something, feel something, vent some of this pent-up frustration. I mean every day I'm waking up, going through the motions and I started to feel numb, like a zombie. At first the pain was intense and it would come in unpredictable waves. And that was okay, I could manage that, you know? But after Pete and then Tre...I'm messed up right now. My emotions are all over the place."

"Have you tried praying?" Dre asked softly.

Standing up from couch, bottle still flush in my palm. "What's that going to do? They're still dead, Dre. They're still gone. Casey's mom had a heart attack in her bathroom. How rude is that!? God is snatching people up and not giving anyone a chance to say goodbye!"

The phone went silent. Dre had never heard me like this before. Tears assembled at the corner of my eyes. I wiped them with the back of my hand and tried not to sniffle.

"The only way is through, Estrell. So, you pray for Grace, for Mercy, for comfort and strength. Pray for peace because it's not going to be easy. Sometimes life knocks you down to your knees…"

"I hear ya, man," I broke in.

"Do you really?"

"Yeah," I reassured. "You're saying I can't hide from this." I walked over to the window and peeked through the blinds. "I'm just tired. I don't like crying. I don't like the faces I make. I can't stand that there's a gaping hole in the middle of my chest and I can't drink enough to fill it. I just want to scream all the time. And on top of that, I have to face the world, don a smile because nobody wants to hear about your problems. Everybody had their own problems to deal with. Man, this is for the birds."

"Alright, man. I know it's been a tough year and I know there's nothing I can say that'll make you feel better. I feel terrible, too. But no one we've lost this year would want to see us still wallowing in this mess. And they definitely wouldn't want us to start a new year off like this. So, here's what I propose, come to church with us on New

Year's Eve. After, we'll go grab a bottle, hit the crib, maybe play some Spades or something. Just hang."

"Who is 'us'?" I tried to bide some time while I thought of a reason to say "no". The last place I wanted to be was church.

"Bruh, ain't none of that important. And I'm not accepting 'no' as an answer. Meet me at Peace Baptist Church off Covington Hwy, 10 o'clock."

Click. Dre was the type of person who would hang up on you. I took another swig and went back to wallowing.

New Year's Eve
10:03 p.m.

The parking lot, packed with sedans and minivans, trucks and trailers looked like a tailgate-for-Jesus party. Dre was on the phone, sitting on the trunk of his car. As I approached, the passenger door flung open and a friend from a past life emerged.

"Estrell," Dre greeted me with our usual high-five, elbow bump, bro hug thing. "Do you remember Kevin?" Dre asked, moving aside.

Shaking his hand, "Hell yeah, I remember Kevin! What's it been? Ten years, man? I say. The level of my excitement was embarrassing but I didn't care.

"Yeah, just about," he answered, smiling.

"Wait, Dre, how do you know this guy?"

"I know everybody, man. But listen, let's run in here and we'll do all the catching up afterwards."

"You're right," I said.

The sanctuary, the overflow room, and the hallway brimmed with people. Luckily, the young adults were having service to themselves, tucked away in the back of the building. It too was standing room only but high-top tables behind the main body of chairs made latecomers feel comfortable. There was a man on stage; probably late twenties, average height, but long and stocky. He could've been the life-size ethnic version of Stretch Armstrong.

We strolled in mid-testimony but it was cool. *Am I tripping?* It seemed like he paused while we got situated but maybe he didn't because no one seemed to notice his voice fade but me. It was a welcoming gesture if he did. It made me feel comfortable. Plus, the man had a kind face, one that said, "I know. It's going to be alright, though."

The room was quiet but it wasn't. Dre and Kev-in went to grab some food and I found a table. When the man began to speak goosebumps tiptoed up my arm and back. The room narrowed and I was alone. A single spotlight, as if atop a light-house, spun in my direction, grazing the top of crowd and came to rest on me. I felt every word.

Brothers and sisters, I know what it is to be lost. I know affliction and pain. I know what it's like to be a believer and not know, to be unable to fathom a mustard seed worth of faith.

I can no longer subscribe to the notion that ignorance is bliss. I used to. To mean, ignorance was the most endearing thing about childhood because you didn't know what was out here, what could kill you.

When you're young, people tell you "anything is possible" and "you can be/ do whatever you want in life" and you believe it. You have no reason not to. There's no reins, no governor, no impediments like experience to throttle your imagination so the possibilities are endless. There is something intrinsically beautiful about that, about having a mind impermeable to the possibility of things going wrong, negative outcomes, or disaster. Ignorance is bliss because you don't know what you don't know. And I envied my peers for their lack of experience because I had seen too much.

When I was child, I had big dreams. I had high hopes forged out of necessity because my family and I were the poorest of poor. A product of a single-parent household, I was the child of an addict. All types of men and women would come and go through our revolving front door and, most nights I was left alone and vulnerable to fend for myself. One night a friend of the family took advantage of that.

Having your innocence snatched away can light a fire inside anyone. I will spare you the gory details of the trauma and just say, as it became more frequent, it made me work harder on the court. And in the classroom. I had to find a way out.

My eyes fixed upon the small man. I listened intently, he had me at mustard seed. I pulled myself away from the message to see if my friends had dialed in as much as I had. They weren't. They hadn't. This solidified my belief that he was speaking to me.

As you can see, I am not a big man. I'm not tall. My hands aren't the size of baseball gloves and my feet aren't the size of Sideshow Bob's. But what I lack in stature and strength, sheer determination made up for. My drive was unmatched. I outworked everybody. Failure wasn't an option. My mind wouldn't allow it. I had to drown out the pain.

I was so angry. You didn't want to see me on the hardwood. You didn't want to guard me alone, so-lo, out there, stuck on an island. I was too quick and nothing was going to stop me. It's funny, deter-mined people always say stuff like that. I convinced myself that what I wanted, God wanted for me too. But you don't know what you don' know, right?

I knew the tracks in my mom's arms made me not want to go home. So, I found ways to stay at the gym. I knew I didn't want to suffer any more so I figured out ways to stay after the school closed. I hid in locker rooms and

closets and when the coast was clear, I prac-
ticed. I practiced and practiced. I watched film
and hit the weight room, because I had big
dreams, you know?

One day, I was going to rise about all this
and you guys were going to see my mean cross-
over on TV. I could see it. I could taste it.
And, after I lead my high school team to vic-
tory in two regional and state championships,
I was one step closer to making that dream of
mine a reality. My plan was working.

College scouts were on me like paparazzi,
calling and stopping by the house. It was cra-
zy. People were sending me gifts and trying to
take me out on the town. I turned it all down,
though. I finally had choices. This is what I
had been praying for. I was not going to ruin
it by doing something foolish. I mean, I was
being recruited by the top schools in the na-
tion, and it felt good to be wanted.

I ended up committing to Duke. I was going
to be a Blue Devil. Unfortunately, two days
before I was scheduled to board a plane, inves-
tigators stopped by the house. They had
pictures of my mom with what they called bag-

*men and apparently, she had accept-ed a cou-
ple of bribes.*

*I hadn't seen her in few weeks. I would stop
by the house on occasion to check on her and
grab clean clothes but mostly I was staying
with friends. Ignorantly, I figured she'd gone
to rehab or something. More than likely, she
had been shacked up with a man. The investigators had a lot of questions. I couldn't tell
them anything and they acted like they didn't
want to believe me. So, the NCAA pulled
my scholarship pending an investigation, and I
was going to have to sit a year out. I was devastated.*

Wow. The story had taken a surprising
turn.

*My coaches and lawyers from the school came
to my aid but there was nothing they could do.
My mother had disappeared and I didn't have
any proof that she wasn't paid for me to play
at Duke. Investigators tore apart my life.
They ransacked the apartment and, despite
me telling them I didn't really live there, they*

found six thousand dollars in a shoebox at the top of the hallway closet. I was screwed.

Now, I need you guys to understand. I wasn't furious at my mother. She had a problem. A problem that had been with her since I could remember so it wasn't at all shocking for her to do something self-serving. However, what did catch me off guard was the nature of the situation she had gotten herself in-to. You see, I found out not only did my mother take money from bag-men known to the NCAA, once she knew people would pay her to sway my college choice, she racked up debt from virtually everyone.

Everything came crashing down. I can go on for days about how deep things got, from the threats on my life and attempting suicide, to finding out my mom had died. That year was the worst year of my life. At rock bottom, I asked God why. I pleaded for a reason. It made no sense. I did all the right things, I stayed out of trouble, I was honest and kind, I never took anything from anyone and yet this was my life. I mean, I prayed and everything!

The room was all but silent now. Teary eyes washed over the faces of men and women alike. The message was just what I needed. For the first time in months, I had clarity. I knew what I was supposed to do. Eagerly, I leaned over and whispered to Kevin, "It's funny how the world works."

God has a way of changing your plans. He has a habit of saying "no" and being quiet in your time of need. I am still struggling with these things. And if I am being honest, it wasn't my intention to share this with you. I wasn't even supposed to be here to-night but when I stepped on stage the Spirit told me all this pain was for you. Someone in here needed to know that they are not alone. Someone needed to know, despite the sore knees and red eyes, all things come together for good. People, the bible says, "... weeping may endure for a night but joy comes in the morning." And with 2015 only moments away, I hope that's tomorrow.

Questions for your consideration

1. Have you ever experienced a life-transforming moment? If so, when and how did it change you?

2. What are some of the author's gifts/talents? Do you share any of those same gifts? How could they be used to benefit others?

3. What were some of the bad choices Estrell made? What were the consequences?

4. The author put himself and others in harm's way several times in this book. How do you think that made him feel?

5. This book is mainly about understanding everyone has a purpose. If you died tomorrow would you have fulfilled yours? How do you want to be remembered?

6. In *Terrible Choices*, Estrell had a real moment when he realized how racism had changed him. How was his thought process wrong? How was it right?

7. What are some of the emotions you experienced while reading this book?

8. Recall a situation where you had to sacrifice something for someone else. Share that story.

9. What is something you would NEVER sacrifice for someone else? And Why?

10. Throughout the book, Estrell claims he was "called to serve". Do you agree? If so, why? If not, why?

11. The author talked about loyalty briefly in *Close Call*. List three principles that matter to you and why.

12. Estrell found himself in some mess several times. In what ways could the author have saved himself from all that trouble?

13. What role did society play in the things that happen to him?

14. Which story resonated with you the most? Why?

15. Did you enjoy this book? Why?

About the Author

Estrell Young III, a published and award-winning poet, author and Baltimore native, is just a God-fearing young man riding a ridiculously mean unicorn. After graduating from the University of West Georgia in 2009 he found himself virtually unemployable due a lengthy criminal history and a DUI arrest he got shortly before graduation. In the months that followed, he battled with depression while devouring bottle after bottle of alcohol until his father had had enough. One morning Estrell Sr. decided to slide a business card under his son's door and instructed him to call the man listed on the front. This one act of love set in motion a comeback of biblical proportions- Estrell interned for free at a local Public Defender's Office for 9 months, Monday through Friday, from open to close, thus showing people who he truly was and that he was not afraid of hard work. He had found his passion in public service and he was rewarded with a job. His writing is merely an extension of that love. do for you? No stranger to stages, his story of redemption is powerful and necessary. God's grace and mercy has covered him from an early age and his journey is eerily like the story of David- arguably one of the best tales in the good book. God, in HIS infinite wisdom sheltered Estrell, hid him away, secluded him from friend and foe until he had nothing but his pen and service to his fellow man

So, what can Estrell. Estrell is currently employed with The Law Office of the Public Defender in Dekalb County, GA. It is here, amongst the invisible, underprivileged, underrepresented, and forgotten, where his story rings the truest, "you are NOT the worst thing you've ever done". And armed with the idea of #ProgressOVRPerfection he wishes to scour the globe and encourage youth to dream big while simply placing one foot in front of the other. If you or your organization are interested in booking Estrell please use one of the links below:

Website: estrellyoungIII.com
Email: authorestrellyoungIII@gmail.com
Instagram: @Iprayedandeverything
FB:www.facebook.com/EstrellYoungIII/

Acknowledgements

13 Brethren, I do not count myself to have apprehended; but one thing I do, forgetting those things which are behind and reaching forward to those things which are ahead, 14 I press toward the goal for the prize of the upward call of God in Christ Jesus.
—Philippians 3: 13-14

This is the most important thing I've ever done. This book, for me, is my greatest accomplishment because it is an offering and I shared it as an act of service. I would be remiss if I didn't acknowledge and thank all the people who have helped me along the way for that reason.

I want to thank my family for all the love and support. Special thanks to my mom for dealing with me and my pseudo OCD- she read these stories more times than I did and I can only imagine how much your brain ached because of it. I love you. To my sister, I love you. You inspire me to be and do...everything. You accomplish and conquer everything and I am proud of the woman you have become. To my father, it may seem like you're absent in these pages but I promise you, you are not. I am the man I am because of the man you are. You taught me things like integrity, loyalty, and compassion. Family has always come first for you and these light post guide me now as I traverse life. You may have not been able to do much but you did more than enough. I love you, pop.

To Casey, you're my guy. You're my brother and I love you. Thank you for all the time and energy you invested in listening to me ramble about dreams and pro-gress and thank you for always believing even when you didn't. I will never forgive you for not telling me I looked like a fool but I do understand why you didn't. I love you and your family.

I want to thank Deondre Lee for invitation to church and being one of the greatest friends one could ask for. I would also like to thank Kevin for sharing that moment with me and being a dear friend. You guys are my brothers.

To Aleeisha Carr, I know we aren't friends anymore but I don't care. Thank you for all the love and support. I am forever indebted to you. I love you for everything and you inspire me.

To Alisa Livan, thank you for making it okay to be a Martian. You are a once-in-a-lifetime friend and I thank you for everything. I love you.

To Dr. Kendra Parker, thank you for all the love and support. Thank you for all the late nights and words of encouragement when I thought I was in over my head and I lacked faith. You are amazing and I am sorry if I never told you.

To the fellas, there's too many of you guys to name but each of you have a special place in my heart. You are all different, valuable, significant and you guys make this world a little more tolerable.

To my Public Defender family, in the Stone Mountain and Alcovy circuits, thank you for putting up with me foolishness. I was able to find myself while doing acts of service and it has been an honor going to battle with each of you every day. Keep up all the excellent work. Valerie, Sabrina, Jennifer, JT, Shemeka, Tish, Lauren, Alpesh, Brian, and LS thank for all your advice and help with this project. It wouldn't be what it is without you.

To Teresa and the Rockdale County ERC, thank you for allowing me to teach and be a tutor. I have learned so much because of you guys and I am grateful. Teresa, I love you and your family. You guys are amazing.

To my friend and editor Julia, thank you for all the love and encouragement. Thank you for being so real and honest with me. Tell your husband and kids I am sorry for whenever I called manic and needy. You guys are amazing and I love you.

To Alexis, there's a special place in my heart for you. Thank you for all your help and the long hours you put in reading this stuff. Your love and encouragement means more than words can express. I love you.

To Janine, you came along toward the end but you've been a bright spot at the end of a chapter.

To my grandpa, this whole journey started with your departure. It's bittersweet because it's completion will bring closure a chapter that will define the rest of my life. I miss you and there isn't a day where you don't cross my mind. I love you to the moon and back.

Finally, I want to thank my entire family and all my friends for every encouraging word and prayer. I love you all and I am not ashamed to say it.

Scriptures
Things I came across along the way

1 The LORD is my shepherd, I lack nothing. 2 He makes me lie down in green pastures, he leads me beside quiet waters, 3 he refreshes my soul. He guides me along the right paths for his name's sake. 4 Even though I walk through the darkest valley, I will fear no evil, for you are with me; your rod and your staff, they comfort me. 5 You prepare a table before me in the presence of my enemies. You anoint my head with oil; my cup overflows. 6 Surely your goodness and love will follow me all the days of my life, and I will dwell in the house of the LORD forever.
— Psalms 23: 1-6 (NIV)

6 Be anxious for nothing, but in everything by prayer and supplication, with thanksgiving, let your requests be made known to God; 7 and the peace of God, which surpasses all understanding, will guard your hearts and minds through Christ Jesus.

—Philippians 4: 6-7 (NKJV)

11 The greatest among you will be your servant.
—Matthew 23:11 (NIV)

9 And He said to me, "My grace is sufficient for you, for My strength is made perfect in weakness." Therefore, most gladly I will rather boast in my infirmities, that the power of Christ may rest upon me. 10 Therefore I take pleasure in infirmities, in reproaches, in needs, in persecutions, in distresses, for Christ's sake. For when I am weak, then I am strong.

—2 Corinthians 12: 9-10 (NKJV)

37 No, in all these things we are more than conquerors through him who loved us. 38 For I am convinced that neither death nor life, neither angels nor demons, [a] neither the present nor the future, nor any powers, 39 neither height nor depth, nor anything else in all creation, will be able to separate us from the love of God that is in Christ Jesus our Lord.
— Romans 8: 37-39 (NIV)

5 For the Lord is good and his love endures forever; his faithfulness continues through all generations.
—Psalms 100: 5 (NIV)

5 Trust in the Lord with all your heart, And lean not on your own understanding; 6 In all your ways acknowledge Him, And He shall direct your paths.

—Proverbs 3: 5-6 (NKJV)

*12 Dear friends, don't be surprised at the
fiery trials you are going through, as if something strange were happening to you. 13
Instead, be very glad—for these trials make
you partners with Christ in his suffering, so
that you will have the wonderful joy of seeing
his glory when it is revealed to all the world.*
—1 Peter 4: 12-13 (NLT)

*7 Instead of your shame you will receive a
double portion, and instead of disgrace you
will rejoice in your inheritance. And so, you
will inherit a double portion in your land, and
everlasting joy will be yours.*

—Isaiah 61: 7 (NIV)

*17 No weapon that is formed against thee shall prosper; and every tongue that shall rise against thee in judgment thou shalt condemn. This is the heritage of the servants of the LORD, and their righteousness is of me, saith the LORD. —**Isaiah 54: 17***

Notes

Notes

Notes